Collecting the Past

Today's libraries and museums are heavily indebted to the passions and obsessions of numerous individual collectors who devoted their lives to amassing collections of books, manuscripts, artworks and other culturally significant objects. *Collecting the Past* brings together the latest research on a wide range of significant British collectors from the eighteenth to the twentieth centuries, including Hans Sloane, Sarah Sophia Banks, Thomas Phillipps, Sydney Cockerell, J. P. Morgan Jr., Alfred Chester Beatty and R. E. Hart.

Contributors to the volume examine the phenomenon of collecting in a variety of settings and across a range of different materials. Considering the aims and motives that led these collectors to assemble such remarkable collections, the book also examines the history of these collections after the collector's death. Particular attention is given to the often complicated relationship between collectors and the public institutions that subsequently came to house their collections. Situated within the framework of cultural collecting more generally, this book offers an authoritative series of essays on key collectors.

Collecting the Past should be most interesting to researchers, academics and postgraduate students engaged in the study of museum studies, book history, manuscript studies, museum history, library history and the history of collecting. Professionals in libraries, museums and galleries will also find the volume of great interest.

Toby Burrows is Senior Researcher at the University of Oxford, UK, and a Senior Honorary Research Fellow at the University of Western Australia.

Cynthia Johnston is Lecturer in the History of the Book and Communications at the Institute of English Studies, School of Advanced Study, University of London, UK.

Collecting the Past

British Collectors and their Collections from the 18th to the 20th Centuries

Edited by
Toby Burrows and Cynthia Johnston

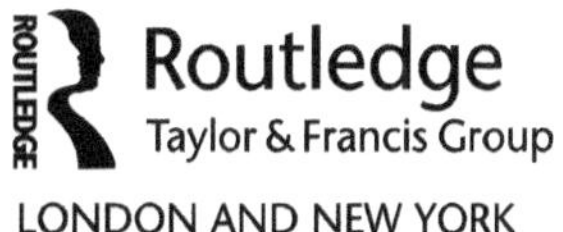

LONDON AND NEW YORK

First published 2019 by Routledge

2 Park Square, Milton Park, Abingdon, Oxfordshire OX14 4RN
52 Vanderbilt Avenue, New York, NY 10017

Routledge is an imprint of the Taylor & Francis Group, an informa business

First issued in paperback 2020

British Library Cataloguing-in-Publication Data
A catalogue record for this book is available from the British Library

Library of Congress Cataloging-in-Publication Data
A catalog record for this book has been requested

ISBN: 978-0-8153-8234-8 (hbk)
ISBN: 978-0-367-60680-0 (pbk)

Typeset in Times New Roman
by ApexCoVantage, LLC

Contents

Figures

Contributors

Karen Attar is the Rare Books Librarian at the University of London's Senate House Library and an Associate Research Fellow of its Institute of English Studies. She has published widely on book collectors and library history, and in 2016 she edited the third edition of the *Directory of Rare Book and Special Collections in the United Kingdom and Republic of Ireland*.

Toby Burrows is Senior Researcher at the Oxford e-Research Centre, University of Oxford, and a Senior Honorary Research Fellow at the University of Western Australia. He has held visiting fellowships at Churchill College, Cambridge, the Free University in Amsterdam, University College London and the University of Pennsylvania. His work on Sir Thomas Phillipps was funded by a European Union Marie Curie International Incoming Fellowship at King's College London (2014–2016).

Laura Cleaver is the Ussher Lecturer in Medieval Art at Trinity College Dublin. She earned her PhD at The Courtauld Institute of Art, University of London. Her most recent book is *Illuminated History Books in the Anglo-Norman World, 1066–1272* (Oxford University Press, 2017), based on research carried out under a Marie Curie Actions Career Integration Grant between 2011 and 2015.

Cynthia Johnston is Lecturer in the History of the Book and Communications at the Institute of English Studies, School of Advanced Study, University of London, where she is also coordinator and course tutor for the MA in the History of the Book. She is also a director of the academic partnership between the Institute of English Studies and the Blackburn Museum and Art Gallery, funded by the Museum between 2015 and 2020. She completed her PhD thesis at the University of London in 2015.

Arlene Leis is an art historian whose research focuses predominately on collections and collecting, cabinets of curiosities, print culture and the inter-relations between art and science. She also has an interest in portraiture, gender studies, dress, sociability and patriotic consumption in the eighteenth century. In 2015 she held a postdoctoral research fellow in the Humanities Research Centre at the University of York, where she completed her PhD thesis.

Danielle Magnusson's doctoral thesis, *Reading the Household: Towards an Economic and Textual Understanding of Early English Drama*, was completed at the University of Washington in 2015. She has since taught in the School of English and worked as a Research Assistant in Trinity College Dublin's Department of History of Art and Architecture on the 'Migrant Manuscripts: the Western Manuscripts of the Chester Beatty Collection' project.

Alice Marples is Research Associate in the John Rylands Research Institute at the University of Manchester. She completed her PhD at King's College London in 2016, on the correspondence of Sir Hans Sloane.

Stella Panayotova has an MA in Classics from the University of Sofia (1990) and a DPhil in medieval history from the University of Oxford (1998). She has been Keeper of Manuscripts and Printed Books at the Fitzwilliam Museum, Cambridge, since 2000, and Director of the *Cambridge Illuminations* research project (since October 2004) and of the *MINIARE* research project (since October 2011).

1 Collecting the past

Manuscript and book collecting in the nineteenth and twentieth centuries

Toby Burrows and Cynthia Johnston

The nineteenth and twentieth centuries were a great age of manuscript and book collecting in Britain and North America. Many of the best-known collectors were active in this period, and several of them founded significant libraries or museums which perpetuate and memorialize their collections to the present day. The turnover of manuscripts alone was at a very high level; the Schoenberg Database of Manuscripts records almost 100,000 transactions through auctions and sales catalogues during this time.[1] This volume, which has its origins in a conference held in 2016 at the Institute of English Studies, School of Advanced Study, University of London, brings together essays on a selection of key people involved in collecting books and manuscripts during this period. While these essays are not intended to form a fully comprehensive history, they aim to illustrate the breadth and variety of collectors and their activities, and demonstrate the various different themes which were at play during this time.

In various ways the history of book and manuscript collecting has parallels in the astonishing growth of the market for artworks in the same period.[2] Many of the key features of that market can also be seen in the world of manuscripts and books. Historic collections in Britain and Western Europe were being sold in the face of changing economic, social and political conditions for aristocratic and landed families. Items from religious houses and churches were acquired, stolen and dispersed, especially in the wake of the suppressions by Napoleon and other rulers in the late eighteenth and early nineteenth centuries. The rapid industrialization of the nineteenth century produced a growing number of extremely wealthy industrialists and bankers, especially in the United States, who felt (or were persuaded to feel) a need to demonstrate their taste, culture and philanthropic commitment through the purchase of rare and expensive books and manuscripts. An increasingly sophisticated infrastructure of dealers, experts and scholars emerged to serve the market; these roles were often blurred and combined, resulting in frequent conflicts of interest. As with the art market, prices for the most desirable items rose to astronomical levels, even as the number of items available for sale contracted. This trend reached its culmination in 2014 when a record price was set for a manuscript volume, with the Rothschild Prayerbook selling at auction for $13.6 million.[3]

The collectors discussed in these essays came from various different backgrounds and collected for different purposes. They range from Sir Hans Sloane, who served as an eighteenth-century precursor of many later developments, and Sarah Sophia Banks, who played an important role alongside her brother Joseph Banks, through to such well-known collectors as Thomas Phillipps, Alfred Chester Beatty and the Morgans, and those who worked with them and for them, like Sydney Cockerell and Belle da Costa Greene. Also covered are R. E. Hart, who exemplifies the regional collecting of northern, industrial Britain, and the hundreds of individual collectors whose collections now form part of the academic and public libraries of Great Britain.

Identifying and reconstructing these collections is not necessarily a straightforward process. In some cases, notably J. Pierpont Morgan and his son Jack (J. P. Morgan Jr.), the collecting fed directly into a public institution established by the collectors themselves (the Morgan Library), and the items they collected – together with the records of their acquisitions – are still together as a collection.[4] Other collections were bequeathed or donated to public institutions, where they have been kept intact. The visiting cards and other printed ephemera collected by Sarah Sophia Banks were donated after her death to the British Museum. R. E. Hart's collections were donated *en bloc* to the Blackburn Public Library, where they remain intact and well documented. The vast collections of Hans Sloane were, for the most part, acquired by the British Museum together with his catalogues and documentation – but not all of the material was retained amid the changing perspectives of the nineteenth century.

In the case of Alfred Chester Beatty, on the other hand, the present-day Chester Beatty Library in Dublin does not reflect the totality of his collecting in the twentieth century. Many of his Western manuscripts were sold off in 1932–1933 and again in 1968–1969. Reconstructing his collections involves painstaking research in the archives of libraries and dealers, as well as through auction and sale catalogues.[5] Thomas Phillipps is an even more extreme case; his huge collection was gradually dispersed in the century after his death in 1872, and is now scattered around the world. The documentation relating to this dispersal is voluminous and complex, and exists in formats ranging from archival documents to printed catalogues to databases of various kinds.[6] The Schoenberg Database of Manuscripts is a particularly valuable starting point for identifying and reconstructing collections like those of Beatty and Phillipps.

One of the features of book and manuscript collecting in the period covered by this volume was the rise of the 'professional' curator and expert, exemplified by such twentieth-century figures as Sydney Cockerell of the Fitzwilliam Museum and Belle da Costa Greene of the Morgan Library, and earlier by Sir Frederic Madden at the British Museum and Henry Bradshaw at the Cambridge University Library. They were not primarily collectors themselves, though Cockerell and Madden certainly dabbled in acquiring their own books and leaves. Instead, they worked to build an institution's collections – as Madden did at the British Museum, and Cockerell at the Fitzwilliam Museum – or they worked closely with one of the wealthy collectors, as Greene did with the Morgans. While they had an impressive degree of knowledge of the history and value of manuscripts, they also had other skills more suited to institutional collection-building. Stella Panayotova shows how Sydney Cockerell was a relentless – and usually successful – practitioner of the art of persuading and influencing wealthy donors, either to give money or to leave their collections to the Fitzwilliam. Laura Cleaver and Danielle Magnusson reveal Belle da Costa Greene's ability to manipulate and negotiate with firms like Quaritch, as well as the value of her talent for persuasion allied with the deep pockets of the Morgans.

There is a tension here between private collecting and public collecting, beginning with Sir Hans Sloane – who, as Alice Marples demonstrates, was deeply concerned that his collections be used and that they be made available for public access. His insistence that they be acquired by the nation and made accessible through the British Museum was one of the driving forces in his frenetic and omnivorous collecting activities.[7] Sir Thomas Phillipps, more than a century later, assembled an equally gigantic collection but failed in his attempts to make it available to more than a few scholarly visitors. As Toby Burrows shows, Phillipps had several similarities with Sloane: absorbing the collections of others, being driven primarily by a desire to preserve the documentary record of the past, and enduring some criticism and ridicule from his contemporaries for his supposed lack of connoisseurship. But he lacked Sloane's talents for influencing and persuading those in power. Phillipps's vast collection was scattered across the globe after his death, and his legacy – unlike Sloane's – is indirect and largely invisible. Some later collectors, such as Alfred Chester Beatty and the Morgans, worked to turn their collections into public institutions as well as personal memorials. Cynthia Johnston demonstrates that others – like R. E. Hart in Blackburn, Lancashire – used their collections to enhance the civic value and importance of their native town.

Karen Attar uses the term 'ossified collections' to identify those handed over to institutional care and maintenance, as opposed to the dynamic nature of collections being formed and added to by private collectors.

This tension can also be seen in the Phillipps manuscript collection; what had been a living and continually growing collection over a period of more than 50 years was split into innumerable pieces after his death and subsumed into many institutional settings.[8] Interestingly, however, a significant number of the items from his collection are still in private hands. The career of Sydney Cockerell is also revealing from this point of view.[9] He worked tirelessly to shape personal, dynamic collections like those of Dyson Perrins and Alfred Chester Beatty, with the long-term goal of turning them into institutional assets, preferably at the Fitzwilliam Museum. Yet even his remarkable talents could not prevent some of these collections from slipping through his fingers.

A striking feature of the activities of many of these collectors was the breadth of their interests. Manuscripts and printed materials were only one aspect of their collecting, in most cases. Sarah Sophia Banks collected coins and medals in addition to the printed ephemera which Arlene Leis discusses here. R. E. Hart also had an extensive coin collection to go with his book collection. Phillipps collected Old Master drawings and paintings, and acted as a patron for two contemporary artists. Cockerell collected paintings and antiquities for the Fitzwilliam. Sloane's books and manuscripts were an adjunct to his huge collection of natural history specimens. In most of the cases covered by this volume, book and manuscript collecting needs to be seen within this broader context of acquisitions across a wide range of different types of material. Even the scope of their manuscript collecting was generally quite broad; Sloane, Phillipps, Beatty and Cockerell were all interested in acquiring manuscripts with origins beyond Western Europe, especially Persia, India and Hispanic America.

None of these collectors worked on their own; they were all part of broader networks of like-minded people, and they all worked their connections vigorously to identify and acquire material. Hans Sloane was part of a global network of suppliers, agents and collectors, and made a crucial contribution to the Royal Society as one of its early Presidents.[10] Sarah Sophia Banks benefited from the extensive social and scientific connections of her brother, Sir Joseph, who was also a long-serving President of the Royal Society.[11] Even Thomas Phillipps made use of a wide circle of dealers and booksellers, and was well-connected with other scholars and antiquarians; he too was a Fellow of the Royal Society.[12] Sydney Cockerell assembled an unrivalled set of patrons, mentors and suppliers, beginning with John Ruskin and William Morris.[13] In a different register, perhaps, R. E. Hart moved in the tight social circles of northern industrialists, as well as having his own connections in the book trade.[14]

The casual observer could be forgiven for thinking that book and manuscript collecting in the nineteenth and earlier twentieth century was dominated by men, with little obvious involvement from women. After all, most of the best-known collectors were men. And yet, as many of these essays show, women played a significant part in this world. In some cases, like Sarah Sophia Banks, they were collectors in their own right, whose collections were housed alongside those of their better-known male relatives. In other cases, like Edith Beatty, they worked with their husbands, making their own acquisitions and (in her case) spending more freely than he did. As for Bella da Costa Greene, she played a crucial role in building the manuscript collection of what became the Morgan Library; the money may have come from the Morgan family, but she was the one who carried out many of the negotiations for the more expensive purchases, and she was the one who built the network of connections with connoisseurs, dealers and owners.[15] Karen Attar shows how many of the special collections now in British libraries were put together by women, sometimes working by themselves and sometimes in collaboration with men. She also reveals that a significant number of collections assembled by men were actually donated to libraries by their female relatives, as some kind of memorial to the collectors.

One of the notable features of the period from the later nineteenth century was the increasing dominance of North American collectors. Laura Cleaver and Danielle Magnusson demonstrate how this worked in the case of the Morgan family, and the alarmed and shocked reaction it provoked in Great Britain. They also discuss the interesting case of Alfred Chester Beatty, who started off as an American mining engineer and ended up as a central figure in the British and Irish collecting world.[16] Nevertheless, British collecting continued to thrive despite the American onslaught, as exemplified by the work of Sydney Cockerell and of collectors like R. E. Hart. As Karen Attar shows, many hundreds of special collections continued to be formed by individual collectors and were subsequently acquired by British libraries during the twentieth century.

Perhaps the most common question asked about these notable collectors was why they collected, and why they collected so obsessively. On the basis of the evidence in this volume, it is clear that there are many answers to this question, and that any one collector may have had multiple reasons for collecting. Undoubtedly, a common element was that collecting manuscripts and other valuable historical objects was a way of demonstrating taste, wealth and social standing. In Great Britain, there was a strong tradition of connoisseurship among the landed gentry, and even new arrivals to this class felt the need to fill their country houses with suitable artistic and literary objects.[17] In the case of the American industrialists and financiers like the Morgans and Beatty, conspicuous expenditure on luxury items was a good way of demonstrating success, taste and wealth. People like

Sydney Cockerell and Belle da Costa Greene were able to make good careers out of advising these collectors and putting their own connoisseurship and knowledge to the best possible use.

In the northern industrial world of someone like R. E. Hart, collecting was closely connected with civic pride and social improvement, as a means of developing the cultural and educational environment of growing regional towns and of giving back to the local community something from the successes of local businesses. This educational element was also connected with the strong thread of antiquarianism, which was probably the main driving force behind the activities of the two most ambitious of our collectors, Hans Sloane and Thomas Phillipps.[18] For both of them, the sheer preservation of as much historical or scientific material as possible was a key goal. Quantity and breadth of collecting were even more important than connoisseurship and selectivity. Securing and transmitting knowledge – or at least its evidentiary base – for the future was the animating factor behind the ceaseless aggregation of their collections. In Sloane's case, this may have been the result of a new-found awareness of the global environment of discovery and science. For Phillipps, it seems to have been an awareness that the evidence for the past – both distant and contemporary – was slipping away and in danger of being lost forever.

However mixed their motives may have been, it is clear that all these collectors felt they were doing important work for posterity. They all seem to have shared a desire to memorialize themselves through their collections, and they seem to have been convinced of the intrinsic value and worth of the manuscripts, books and other materials they were collecting. Ultimately, that memorial was best expressed in the 'ossified' setting of a public institution, whether by setting up one's own institution (as Jack Morgan did with his library), or by shaping an institution to reflect one's own taste and discernment (as Cockerell did with the Fitzwilliam Museum) or simply by donating to an existing institution (as R. E. Hart did). In this way, the history of private collecting dovetails into the wider history of collecting by museums, galleries, archives and libraries.[19] Together they illuminate the social processes through which objects have been selected, preserved and arranged to educate, illustrate and capture the knowledge of the world and the memory of the past.

Notes

1 https://sdbm.library.upenn.edu/ (accessed 14 May 2018).

2 Joseph Alsop, *The Rare Art Traditions: The History of Art Collecting and Its Linked Phenomena Wherever These Have Appeared* (New York: Harper & Row, 1982).

3 www.christies.com/lotfinder/Lot/the-rothschild-prayerbook-a-book-of-hours-5766082-details.aspx (accessed 14 May 2018).
4 Jean Strouse and Charles E. Pierce, Jr., eds., *The Morgan Library: An American Masterpiece* (New York: Morgan Library, 2000).
5 Laura Cleaver, 'The Western Manuscript Collection of Alfred Chester Beatty (ca. 1915–1930),' *Manuscript Studies*, 2.2 (Fall 2017), 445–482.
6 Toby Burrows, 'The History and Provenance of Manuscripts in the Collection of Sir Thomas Phillipps: New Approaches to Digital Representation,' *Speculum*, 92.S1 (October 2017), S39–S64.
7 James Delbourgo, *Collecting the World: The Life and Curiosity of Hans Sloane* (London: Allen Lane, 2017).
8 A. N. L. Munby, *The Dispersal of the Phillipps Library* (Phillipps Studies No. 5) (Cambridge, UK: Cambridge University Press, 1960).
9 Stella Panayotova, *I Turned It into a Palace: Sydney Cockerell and the Fitzwilliam Museum* (Cambridge: Fitzwilliam Museum, 2008).
10 Delbourgo, *Collecting the World.*
11 John Gascoigne, *Joseph Banks and the English Enlightenment: Useful Knowledge and Polite Culture* (Cambridge: University Press, 1994).
12 A. N. L. Munby, *The Formation of the Phillipps Library Up to the Year 1840* (Phillipps Studies, No. 3) (Cambridge, UK: Cambridge University Press, 1954); A. N. L. Munby, *The Formation of the Phillipps Library from 1841 to 1872* (Phillipps Studies, No. 4) (Cambridge, UK: Cambridge University Press, 1956).
13 Panayotova, *I Turned It into a Palace.*
14 Cynthia A. Johnston and Sarah J. Biggs, eds., *Blackburn's Worthy Citizen: The Philanthropic Legacy of R. E. Hart* (London: Institute of English Studies, 2013).
15 Heidi Ardizzone, *An Illuminated Life: Belle da Costa Greene's Journey from Prejudice to Privilege* (New York: W. W. Norton & Company, 2007).
16 Arthur J. Wilson, *The Life & Times of Sir Alfred Chester Beatty* (London: Cadogan Publications, 1985).
17 Mark Purcell, *The Country House Library* (New Haven: Yale University Press, 2017).
18 On the subject of antiquarianism more broadly, see: Peter N. Miller, *History and Its Objects: Antiquarianism and Material Culture since 1500* (Ithaca: Cornell University Press, 2017); Robin Myers and Michael Harris, eds., *Antiquaries, Book Collectors, and the Circles of Learning* (New Castle: Oak Knoll Press, 1996).
19 Sarah Longair, ed., 'Cultures of Curating: The Limits of Authority,' special issue, *Museum History Journal*, 8.1 (January 2015), 1–117; Caroline Brown, ed., 'Memory, Identity and the Archival Paradigm,' special issue, *Archival Science*, 13.2/3 (June 2013), 85–272.

2 Creating and keeping a national treasure

The changing uses of Hans Sloane's collection in the eighteenth century

Alice Marples

No account of British collecting can be considered complete without some discussion of the remarkable life and collections of Sir Hans Sloane (1660–1753). Across a lifetime spanning over 90 years, this relatively under-appreciated Irish-born physician and naturalist amassed one of the greatest collections of the early modern period. Sloane's collection contained thousands upon thousands of objects of all descriptions: Guinean ivory bracelet rattles, the earliest and largest English astrolabe to have survived from the Middle Ages, a seventeenth-century herbal of East Indian plants, Japanese slippers, narwhale tusks and hornbill skulls, and a 1543 vellum copy of Andreas Vesalius' *De Humani Corporis Fabrica*. Such wonders figuratively sat alongside less exciting items, such as soil specimens, rusty nails or bits of old bone; the portrait of the infamous 'pirate' William Dampier that Sloane had commissioned (to some surprise) staring down those of more traditionally acceptable worthies and expensive gemstone cameos nestled in amongst scraps of waste paper and old prescriptions.

Sloane's contemporaries were aware of the value of his collection. In a speech at his funeral given by the Bishop of Bangor, it was said:

> That a treasure like to this never was amass'd together, is beyond a doubt: all that is call'd great in its kind in the world becomes contemptible by comparison; nor can we imagine that such an one ever can be compil'd again, unless such another almost miraculous combination of causes should appear to give it origin.[1]

In his will, Sloane offered the collection to the nation for £20,000 (a fraction of its true worth) with instructions that, if Britain did not want it, it was to be offered to a series of European scientific institutions before the idea of splitting the collection was to be considered. When George II refused the offer, Parliament raised a public lottery to finance the purchase, stating that it should 'be preserved intire without the least diminuation or separation' so that 'the said *Museum* or collection may be preserved and maintained, not only for the inspection and entertainment of the learned and curious, but for the general use and benefit of the publick.'[2] The first 'national public museum in the world' thus opened its doors to 'the people' in 1759, representing what Kim Sloan has described as 'one of the most potent acts of the Enlightenment.'[3]

The creation of Sloane's collection fits within a long tradition of broad-ranging natural history collecting reaching back to the Renaissance. Humanistic 'Cabinets of Curiosities' or 'theatres of nature' displaying a wealth of exotic or wonderous objects which were hard to obtain and difficult to understand, symbolized not only the glory of God's craft and the intricacy of nature, but also the accumulated knowledge and utility of individual naturalists. Royal and aristocratic cabinets were similarly constructed in order to proclaim the wealth and learning of the patron and their dominance over society.[4] The creation of collections in the early modern period was usually bound up with structures of power and authority, the representation of systems of the world and the structures of aristocratic or scholarly society, which accumulated value and esteem. But though Sloane's collection certainly functioned in this way, it also contained vast amounts of far less glamorous materials, such as the 12,000-odd glass-fronted boxes of vegetable substances, or more mundane everyday items such as old medical advertising bills.[5] This apparent attempt to 'collect the world' – drawing materials from across the face of the globe and seeking to *rationalize* it, to place it in order through classification, thereby working towards the creation of an encyclopedic resource for the improvement of knowledge – represents a shift in cultures of British collecting from the scholarly 'virtuoso' tradition into an arguably more commercial, political and definitely more public-facing enterprise.[6] Even before his death and bequest, Sloane's private collection had come to be associated with 'the nation.' This chapter will demonstrate that such a shift in the function and meaning of this collection developed both organically and quite deliberately from the changing ways in which it was used by contemporaries, and will show how these intertwined with Sloane's public identity and social importance.[7] The 'almost miraculous causes' were, to a great extent, the specific time, place and politics Sloane inhabited and, above all, the new, self-conscious attitude towards knowledge creation and communication that it developed.

Sloane's collection began quite humbly. Always interested in nature as a boy, he began collecting early, and trained first as an apothecary and then as a physician. Yet he claimed that it was his election as a Fellow of the Royal Society in 1685 that first incited him to 'do what [he] could to be no useless Member, but to cast [his] Mite towards the Advancement of Natural

Knowledge and the Faculty of Physic, and by that means endeavour to deserve a Place amongst so many Great and Worthy Persons.'[8] He therefore leapt at the chance to travel to Jamaica as the personal physician to the Duke of Albemarle in 1687, despite being warned off by various friends and mentors, including the esteemed reverend naturalist John Ray: 'Many of the Antient and best Physicians having travelled to the Places whence their Drugs were bought, to inform themselves concerning them.'[9] Though the Duke died within a year of taking up his governorship on that island (through no fault, it must be said, of his young physician), Sloane made endless observations and collections around the island, recording case histories of illnesses and treatments on the plantations, and gathering over 800 botanical specimens to bring home.[10] Once back in England, and advantageously married to Elizabeth Rose (née Langley), the rich widow of a sugar plantation owner, he set up a highly successful medical practice. He worked to produce a catalogue of the plants he had brought back, publishing this in 1696, as well as the highly detailed account of his travels published in two volumes in 1707 and 1725, for an extremely eager audience. As John Ray wrote to him in May 1692:

> I have been importunate with you to hasten the publication of your Discoveries in your History of Nature, as well for the Advancement of reall knowledge, & gratification of the Learned & inquisitive, as for your own deserved honour … I am glad you make such progresse, & cannot but approve your deliberation & circumspection: and agree with [^you] that the clearing up of difficulties, & reconciling of Authors, & reducing & settling the severall histories & relations of ['things' crossed out] species, will be a thing of eminent use, & of as much advantage to the Reader as pains to the Author.[11]

Collecting in this way offered a remedy to the material and epistemological instability of early modern botanical and medical inquiry, at the complicated crossroads between the 'old' or Ancient knowledge and theories based on the 'New Method.' As one frustrated chemist put it in 1675, he had

> lived long enough (almost forty years acquainted with this Art) to see it by improvement in all points turned topsie-turvie, the old Learning belonging to it exploded by Scholars themselves, the old Education in Academies judged incompetent, the places themselves being too narrow to afford much observation or experience, and the manner of life more speculative and notional than Mechanick or laborious.[12]

Increasingly aware of all that they did not know in the world, European medics and naturalists sought to obtain the widest range of source materials that they could, driving trade with the aim of testing old knowledge and verifying new information.[13] As Sloane's friend, fellow collector and agent, the apothecary James Petiver, wrote to one Captain John Walduck in Barbados:

> It is, Sir, to such Curious Persons as your selfe that we at this distance must owe what your parts of the late discovered World can afford us. Your residence there may give us great light into many things which we as yet but imperfectly know and others we are totally ignorant of, by gathering things in all seasons and consequently in their severall states of growth or vegetation by which we shall be able to give better description and more accurate Figures of them.[14]

Sloane was one of many Europeans collecting anything and everything natural that they could lay their hands on, through all sort of channels and across lengthening chains of commercial or unknown intermediaries. The emphasis was on obtaining the material, and then figuring out what to do with it, swapping and sharing resources according to requirements. Sloane's extensive correspondence reveals the great encouragement given to individuals to send collectors material, whether for money or for social credit. With demand so high, even duplicates held great value, being circulated through professional and sociable networks until they became useful, for example:

> I'm looking over my Plants and Separating the Duplicates, I have made up this small Collection for you … I send some of the same sort to Misters Rand and Miller, and which I must request to exchange for some Specimens in the Dendrology in which my Hortus Siccus is very deficient. If any should be wanting, of which they have no duplicates, I desire I may be Supplyed from you.[15]

Sloane, as a collector sitting at the intersection of an increasing number of scholarly and commercial networks, and with contacts around the world, was regularly called on to supply specimens, contacts or recommendations regarding materials or individuals who would be of use to natural inquiry. Fellow physicians would write to him, asking him for his opinion on the results of their experiments, or sending him various curious things extracted from various curious bodies. Botanists would write to ask him to patronize their publications, travellers to finance their ventures, mechanics to approve of their scientific instruments, chemists of their new techniques. Sloane accumulated objects as by-products of such inquiries, as individuals sent him gifts in return for favours or for the use of his collection, which grew with every communication.[16]

In his role as Secretary (1693–1713) and then President (1727–1741) of the Royal Society, Sloane funnelled resources into the Society, using his wealth, private networks and collections to bolster the institution as it struggled with its fortunes in the early eighteenth century.[17] Most visibly of all, he filled the pages of the Society's journal, the *Philosophical Transactions*, with the epistolary materials sent to him.[18] Keenly aware of both the individual and institutional benefits of encouraging such communication, Sloane actively canvassed for correspondents both privately and as Secretary:

> The Royal Society are resolved to prosecute vigorously *the whole design of their institution*, and accordingly they desire you will be pleased to give them an account of what you meet with or hear of, that is curious in nature, or *in any way* tending to the advancement of natural knowledge, or useful arts. They in return will always be glad to serve you *anything in their power.*[19]

He made a statement of the general usefulness of circulating knowledge, in whatever form, in the preface to the 1699 *Transactions*:

> There is no doubt but the more discerning will make a great difference between what is related in [the *Transactions*] as Matter of Fact, Experiment, or Observation, and what is *Hypothesis*. The first sort of Relations (of which all these Papers contain, some) are, and must always be useful, and the latter may be pass'd over by such as dislike them.

Those, he stated, included himself, but he understood that 'future Accidents, and Observations, will make them go off, and be hereafter succeeded by others more plausible.'[20]

In this, Sloane was echoing the call of the times, the 'culture of conversation' that was being fostered in the coffeehouses, 'penny universities' and print culture of the time, and aligning the Royal Society with the understanding that knowledge should be readily available and easily digested, shared and discussed, ideally by a broad socially mixed group (although this was not always desirable in practice). Journals such as *The Athenian Mercury*, *The Spectator*, *The Tatler* and *The Ladies' Diary*, alongside other forms of print culture, were industriously constructing the concept of a fashionable (and profitable) 'political public' by directing, engaging with, and then reflecting back the ideal of a literate, liberal and self-reflective nation that could and would hold the state to account.[21] The facilitation of information exchange and wider learning was increasingly perceived as a way to create a stronger nation, and this took on a distinct cultural and political role in the early eighteenth century. Individuals were encouraged to gather, communicate and utilize knowledge in order to improve themselves and those around them: in so doing, they believed they were demonstrating their 'public spirit' by improving the state and, in so doing, gaining valuable social credit. Sloane himself emphasized these aspects of his public activities, stating that 'he very freely & with great civility shewed [his collection] to his own Country men and strangers to the advancement of the Glory of God, the honour & renown of his Country & the no small promotion of knowledge and usefull arts.'[22] The religious and intellectual reasons Sloane gave for taking the time and trouble to amass and disseminate his collections are unsurprising, as they had long been a feature of scholarly discourse regarding 'microcosmic' collections. What is unusual here is that Sloane specifically mentioned that he was motivated to share his private collections broadly with his own 'Country men and strangers' for the 'honor & renown of his Country.'

In this way, collecting was increasingly conceived of as a work of national, public service, as a letter from Thomas Hearne to Sloane in 1721 demonstrates:

> I am very sensible of your great Treasure, and, if I should come to London (where I never was yet) I would endeavour to make my self better acquainted with it, especially since there is so much in it about Antiquity. I wish Catalogues of such noble Libraries and Museums as yours were published. Twoud be of great service to Learning, especially if the Owners were, like yourself, of true publick Spirit.[23]

Circulating libraries and book clubs were formed for this end, and provincial societies and universities alike sought to establish their own collections. So Edward Lhwyd wrote to Sloane from Oxford in 1701:

> I am order'd by Dr Mander our present Vice Chancellr to give you ... the Thanks of the University for the continuance of your Favours by your late Promise to Dr Hicks for bestowing on this museum some Part of your Duplicats. ... In general you may be well assur'd any thing you please to Spare us. ... Here are already two cabinets of Dr Plot's, one of Dr Lister's, and one or two of another person's. And I think it most proper that yours be also reposited in a Distinct Cabinet, which though you should not furnish immediately; you may perhaps hereafter be mindfull of, as occasion shall offer. I shall take care to register your Donation according to our usual manner.[24]

The growing cultural fixation on 'useful information' and public education had an impact on the ways in which many individual collectors conceived and prepared for the future of their collections. Though some European collections, such as that of Govert Bidloo, were not designed to last for centuries, but rather be thrown away after use, many collectors worked to ensure that their collections would continue to be used after their death.[25] William Courten, for example, bequeathed his collection to his friend Sloane, despite the fact that it contained a number of objects which might not have interested Sloane, who seems only to have been collecting natural historical objects at that point. Carol Gibson-Wood has suggested that 'the impetus for his expansion into coins, medals, prints, drawings and other areas may well have come from his acquisition of Courten's "Museum" in 1702.'[26] Using his collection, Sloane continued to exchange money and objects with Courten's correspondents such as the Scottish botanist James Sutherland and John Lely, son of the artist and collector, Sir Peter.[27]

Leaving collections to friends or fellow collectors was designed to ensure the continuance of valuable individual correspondence networks, relationships of exchange built up over lifetimes using particular sets of resources, preserving the links between the collections and the scholarly work that was done on them. As Charles Preston wrote: 'I am very well pleased that Mr Charleton has left his collections in the hands of one who knows so well how to put a value on them, and I very much approve of your resolution of keeping them together.'[28] As P. S. Morrish notes:

> As early as December 1683, about eighteenth months after [a] visit to [Henry] Chetham's, Ralph [Thoresby] was examining property deeds 'for a Cottage adjoining my garden where I have some thoughts … to build a public library, and a better conveniency for the collection of rarities which are now disadvantageously crowded up.' That phrase 'public library,' of course, had nothing to do with rate-supported libraries in the nineteenth-century sense, but echoed Oxbridge usage; it would be a library to which respectable and capable people might resort.[29]

In the event, however, Thoresby vacillated over his will to such an extent that his death on 16 October 1725 caused a great deal of scholarly anxiety. Thomas Hearne wrote to Richard Richardson 'hoping that the [book] collection would fall into good hands and suggesting that it might join that of Sir Hans Sloane.'[30] Unfortunately, however, such plans were never realized, and Thoresby's collection was broken up and dispersed to such an extent that few items have since been able to be traced (although some have very recently resurfaced).[31] There was no guarantee for the security of a collection after the death of the collector: promises could be forgotten, wills could be lost, and trusted friends and relatives could easily find their fortunes compromised by circumstances forcing them to sell.

When an important collector died, and particularly when remarkable or useful collections found their way onto the public market through auction (rather than, for example, being deposited into a public institution), a flurry of worried letters circulated.[32] Sloane received several letters regarding the sale of the eminent physician Francis Bernard's library in 1698, including one from William Sherard, who wrote from Rome with a huge list of books he had managed to procure or intended to obtain for Sloane: 'I hear by the Gazette that Dr Bernard's library is to be sold by Auction Oct 4th & hope this will be with you time enough to not buy there what I have for you already.'[33] There is every chance that this did not happen, as Thomas Godwin wrote to Sloane the following January to say that he had desired to obtain a specific book at Dr Bernard's auction, but it had gone so fast he missed it: understanding that Sloane had bought it, but already owned a copy, he asked if Sloane would transfer it to him in return for a crown.[34] Similarly, when Robert Sibbald was preparing for the press the catalogue of the library of Sir James Balfour, he repeatedly asked Sloane if he wanted anything from the collection of this man who, along with his brother Andrew, should be considered 'great promoters and Advancers of the Best and most Curious Learning in the Kingdom.' Charles Preston likewise sent Sloane a Balfour catalogue in the hopes that he would be interested in acquiring things from it.[35]

Because of his wealth, connections and knowledge, Sloane was relied upon to intervene in situations where valuable collections or material useful to scholars or the public might otherwise be lost. Innumerable letters were written to Sloane to ask for information or advice regarding specific auctions, or else to inform him of them in the hope that he might secure material. People knew that Sloane had the power to bring material into Britain from abroad, and to distribute it usefully: John Macky, for example, wrote from Bruges in 1710 to inform Sloane of the death of a man there, enclosing a catalogue:

> This Collection is to be sold Entire & I believe that Cheap, or if a Pass could be obtained from the Custom House of London, for bringing them over, One of the Heirs would carry them thither, for the curious to be Satisfied. As you are Curious in those things your self, & acquainted with those of the Royal Society that would be glad of such a Purchase; I send you the Book which contains so many Various things as takes up seven hours to see, If one will Examine every thing that's shown.[36]

Archibald Adams similarly wrote to inform Sloane of his correspondence with Frederik Ruysch over the selling of his museum, and proposed a collective clubbing together in order to purchase it:

> I had another Epistle from Dr Ruysch about his museum in which he tells me he had rather dispose of it here than any where els byt I belive no English man will sooner engage in that purchase than your self whose judgment & abilities bear a proportion to the value you have for such sort of knowledge, My opinion … is that it may be very easily purchas't thus. Every physician in and about London to subscribe 20 & Surgeon 30, because it more immediately concern them besides the voluntary contributions of others, which would soon amount to the value requir'd.[37]

Here, it appears Sloane was being asked to organize a joint-stock company in order to obtain material for the good of the medical and scientific community (though not limited to them alone). Furthermore, that the acquisition of this material is linked to a competitive sense of national intellectual culture, as Adams goes on to say:

> If it should take England would soon outdo all the world, Ruysch tells me that if any British Subject corporation or College shall purchase his closet he will make me as perfect as himself in the art of Embalming Inspecting & preserving in animated body. … It would soon make Gresham on[e] of the finest anatomical repositorys in the world which I would willingly undertake purely to promote the designs of publick benefactors.

In this way, Sloane's collection not only facilitated but also conserved the collections of the country: in 1710, for example, he acquired Leonard Plukenet's collection, Englebert Kaempfer's in 1717, and James Petiver's in 1718. In so doing he preserved the productions of British scholarly activity while simultaneously adding those of foreign efforts.[38] In this, perhaps, we see the beginnings of the idea of the rescue of objects and knowledge which Constance Classen and David Howe have ascribed to a certain mode of nineteenth-century colonial collecting.[39] Certainly the 'rescuing' of knowledge had a long history. Sir Hugh Platt, for example, a contemporary of Francis Bacon (and, according to Deborah Harkness, influential colleague) had been fascinated in the sixteenth century by the myriad methods of knowledge production he saw in the city around him, and worked hard to collect and collate, giving as much time to the intelligence of housewives as he did to guild-masters in his endeavour. Sloane, who came to own

88 volumes of Platt's collections of secrets and 'rustic' recipes (medical, chemical, alchemical and cosmetic), certainly shared this strong general appreciation for the preservation and processing of knowledge.[40]

Yet it is not incidental that Sloane's collection of other collections was occurring in the same period that saw the rise of scholarly historicism (the assertion by the scholarly community of its own history) alongside increasing topographical and antiquarian enquiry, contributing towards wide-ranging debates on the nature of the historic 'English' identity within post-Union political and literary realms, as well as within the context of increasingly aggressive colonization and empire.[41] Collections such as Sloane's must therefore be understood within the context of a distinctive rhetorical culture of accessible public knowledge-sharing for an increasingly associational and moralizing British public.

For, as it grew and grew, Sloane's collection became a 'must-see' attraction for any visitor to London. It even featured in Edward Hatton's *New View of London* (London, 1708), which proclaimed in its preface to

> afford Satisfaction and Pleasure to Readers of all Tempers and Complexions, and the whole will be found a Treatise properly adapted to the use of all such English Nobles and Gentlemen, as intend to Travel, whereby they may be enabled, when in Foreign Countries, to give a Satisfactory Account of the Metropolis of their own.[42]

Increasing numbers of individuals, whether known to Sloane or not, used his collection for the purposes of furthering their own networks, as when the Italian opera librettist, composer, theatre manager and numismatist, Nicola Francesco Haym, requested access for 'This Learned Gentleman … sent a traveling by his Master the Prince of Saze Gortha [Saxe-Gotha], to see the Libraries & Curiosities in England & other parts; and desiring particularly to see your famous Collection.'[43] In the *Weekly Journal, or Saturday's Post* of the 25 May 1723, it was reported that: 'Several Foreign Ministers went, last Week, to see Sir Hans Sloane's extraordinary Collection of natural and artificial Curiosities, and were extremely well pleased therewith.'[44] Robert Hales of the Council Office wrote to Sloane from St. James Place in January 1709, and asked whether several European 'Strangers of Distinction' might allowed into his 'Curious Cabinet': 'I hope Sir you'l pardon the freedom I take: since it proceeds from an ardent desire of making your Name & Merits known in Foreign parts as well as at Home.'[45] Hales wrote again in 1718 to ask whether more strangers from abroad could see it, saying that visitors who did not see Sloane's cabinet when they came to England 'are ashamed to leave this Kingdom.'[46]

Sloane and his collection were seen to be worthy of international celebration, representative of British learning and its growing political and cultural power. It was favourably compared with others found abroad, because of its size, range and value. The Leeds merchant and antiquarian, Ralph Thoresby, described his visit in early June 1701:

> Dr Sloane (now Sir Hans) in whose inestimable museum I was most courteously entertained many a pleasant hour, he has a noble library, too large rooms, well stocked with valuable manuscripts and printed authors, an admirable collection of dried plants from Jamaica. ... He gave me the printed catalogue and some Indian seeds, he has other curiosities without number, and above value; Bishop Nicholson (who is a competent judge, having been in those parts) says, it vastly exceeds those of many foreign potentates, which are so celebrated in history.[47]

Thoresby visited again on 28 May 1721:

> at Dr Sloane's, who entertained us most agreeably in his incomparable museum, any one branch whereof, whether relating to manuscripts or printed authors, antiquities, or natural curiosities, was sufficient to entertain the most curious person for a long time. My Lord Bishop of Carlisle [Nicholson], who is a most competent judge, (having seen many foreign repositories) writ me that those of the great princes beyond seas, are as rivulets to this ocean.[48]

Once again, princely cabinets abroad – and any scholarly or courtly reliance upon them – are dismissed in favour of Sloane's, which was itself represented as being larger and more open and, therefore, of much greater worth. The understanding of national identity and public culture in England at this time was perceived to be in opposition to the supposed excessive centralization of the absolutist continent, particularly after the lapse of the Licensing Act in England in 1696 (in contrast to the increasingly strong system of censorship by the French state) and during the War of Spanish Succession (1701–1714). The looseness, voluntarism and relatively unregulated nature of natural enquiry in England was specifically related by contemporaries to other attitudes regarding politics and the nature of social organization.[49] Sloane's collection was understood to represent the diverse and dedicated endeavours of the nation and, in preserving the distinctive vitality, idiosyncrasy and social mixture of its discursive intellectual culture, allowed for the better encouragement of inquiry. This is something which Thomas Birch particularly emphasizes in his famous memoir of Sloane:

> The Treasure, which he bequeath'd to his Country, & which is now purchas'd for it by the Parliament, may be attended with *numberless Advantage* to the Public. Here, the young Physician, Chemist, & Apothecary may become well acquainted with every Substance, Vegetable, or Mineral, <that is ever> employ'd in Medicine. The Curious in Ores & Metals, by viewing Specimens of every sort, will be instructed in what Beds of Stone or other Matter they are usually found, & by that Means will be inabled to judge what Metal's or Metallic Bodies the Rocks or Mountains, which they examine, may probably contain; whereby rich Mines, with which Great Britain unquestionably abounds, may more easily be discover'd. Even the Clays, Okers, Sands, Stones, Marbles, Earths &c. may lead to the finding better Materials for the Potter, the Painter, the Glass-maker, the Lapidary, & many other Artists, to improve their Manufactures.[50]

The idea of 'numberless advantage' is key here, reflecting a wider sense of knowledge at the time, one that aligned the communication of information for unknown ends with general, providential progress and profit.[51] Everything in the universe – from wonders and systems of nature to the science of man, and from the inner workings of the heart to the body politic – was ultimately knowable. But to know would require immense amounts of energy, discussion and coordination. By keeping together all the achievements of man's accumulated knowledge, from whatever source and in whatever format, and preserving the connections between different endeavours, Birch saw that Sloane's collection could help achieve this goal:

> In short, the Naturalist will find in this Musaeum almost every thing, which he can wish, & will be greatly assisted in his Inquiries & Observations by the Catalogue of it in 38 Volumes in fol. & 8 in quarto, containing short Accounts of every particular, with Reference to the Authors, who have treated them.[52]

The collection – originally pursued in the course of largely private and professional ends – steadily became a tool of both social preservation and communal representation. In connecting a wide range of private and institutional enterprise, the collection could inspire and aid all those who wished to create knowledge, whether for their own intellectual and moral improvement, their desire to contribute to the public benefit or their wish to capitalize on the commercial and associational nature of information exchange. It also represented the diversity of purposes, interests and experiences thought to be intrinsic to the health and progress of society, something which was increasingly thought to set the public of Britain apart from the rest of Europe. In this way, Sloane's collection was configured by contemporaries as a paragon of British society and an example of its exceptionalism. Its power was configured in terms of all those who felt they had aided its creation, and the growing concept of a British 'public' they felt they were serving in doing so. The 'almost miraculous combination of causes' was the fundamental qualities that ensured the transformation of Sloane's private 'scholarly' collection into a public, institutional one. Collections were increasingly seen as shared resources for the facilitation of many different kinds of inquiry. The institutionalization of Sloane's collection as the new British Museum should therefore be seen as both a departure in purpose as well as a natural development of use, consciously reflecting both the scientific reputation and the growing international wealth of a newly consolidated Britain.

Sloane's legacy in the world of book and manuscript collecting – as opposed to natural history and the sciences – is difficult to determine. The universal scope and range of his collections may have inspired Sir Thomas Phillipps in the nineteenth century, though there is no explicit evidence of this.[53] More obviously influential seems to have been Sloane's insistence on public access to his collections and eventual public ownership of them. In the nineteenth century, and certainly by the early twentieth century, there was increasing agreement that collectors who wanted to preserve their collections for posterity and who felt some obligation to the public good should either make a bequest to a public institution or establish such an institution themselves.[54] In these ways, Sloane influenced the later history of collecting, even as his own collection became increasingly neglected in its British Museum home.

Notes

1 London, British Library, Add. MS 6269, f.266: Zachary Pearce, 'A Sermon preached at the funeral of Sir Hans Sloane Jan 18th. 1753.' This quotation opens the most recent (and most extensive) contribution to the growing body of work on Sloane: James Delbourgo, *Collecting the World: The Life and Curiosity of Hans Sloane* (London: Allen Lane, 2017). See also: Alison Walker, Arthur MacGregor and Michael Hunter, eds., *Books to Bezoars: Sir Hans Sloane and His Collections* (London: British Library, 2012).

2 Quoted in Anne Goldgar, 'The British Museum and the Virtual Representation of Culture in the Eighteenth Century,' *Albion*, 32.2 (2000), 199–200.

3 Kim Sloan and Andrew Burnett, eds., *Enlightenment: Discovering the World in the Eighteenth Century* (London: British Museum, 2003), p. 13.

4 Paula Findlen, *Possessing Nature: Museums, Collecting, and Scientific Culture in Early Modern Italy* (London: University of California Press, 1994); Lorraine Daston and Katherine Park, *Wonders and the Order of Nature, 1150–1750*

(New York: Zone Books, 1998); Oliver Impey and Arthur MacGregor, eds., *The Origins of Museums: The Cabinet of Curiosities in Sixteenth- and Seventeenth-Century Europe* (Oxford: Clarendon, 2001); Brian W. Ogilvie, *The Science of Describing: Natural History in Renaissance Europe* (Chicago: University of Chicago Press, 2006).

5 Victoria R. M. Pickering, 'Putting Nature in a Box: Hans Sloane's "Vegetable Substances" Collection' (unpublished doctoral thesis, Queen Mary University of London, 2017); Arnold Hunt, 'Sloane as a Collector of Manuscripts,' in Walker, *Books to Bezoars*.

6 Charles W. J. Whithers, 'Geography, Natural History, and the Eighteenth-Century Enlightenment: Putting the World in Its Place,' *History Workshop Journal*, 39 (1995), 136–163; Ken Arnold, *Cabinets for the Curious: Looking Back at Early English Museums* (Aldershot: Ashgate, 2000); Richard Drayton, *Nature's Government: Science, Imperial Britain, and the 'Improvement' of the World* (New Haven: Yale University Press, 2000); Craig Ashley Hanson, *The English Virtuoso: Art, Medicine, and Antiquarianism in the Age of Empiricism* (Chicago: University of Chicago Press, 2009).

7 Barbara M. Benedict, 'Collecting Trouble: Sir Hans Sloane's Literary Reputation in Eighteenth-Century Britain,' *Eighteenth-Century Life*, 36.2 (2012), 111–142.

8 Hans Sloane, *A Voyage to the Islands of Madera, Barbados, Nieves, S. Christophers, and Jamaica, with the Natural History . . . of the Last of Those Islands* (London, 1707), preface.

9 *Ibid.*

10 Delbourgo, *Collecting the World*, Chapter 2: 'Island of Curiosities.'

11 London, British Library, Sloane MS 4036, f. 123: John Ray to Hans Sloane (25 May 1692, Black Notley).

12 Adrian Huyberts, *A Corner-Stone Laid towards the Building of a New Colledge* (London, 1675), pp. 9–10.

13 Harold J. Cook, *Matters of Exchange: Commerce, Medicine and Science in the Dutch Golden Age* (New Haven: Yale University Press, 2007); Pratik Chakrabarti, *Materials and Medicine: Trade, Conquest and Therapeutics in the Eighteenth Century* (Manchester: Manchester University Press, 2010); Alice Marples and Victoria R. M. Pickering, 'Patron's Review: Exploring Cultures of Collecting in the Early Modern World,' *Archives of Natural History*, 43.1 (2016), 1–20.

14 London, BL, Sloane MS 3337, f. 135: James Petiver to John Walduck (1 January 1711, London).

15 London, BL, Sloane MS 4053, f. 213: Thomas Shaw to Hans Sloane (12 May 1734, Oxford).

16 James Delbourgo, 'Listing People,' *Isis*, 103.4 (2012), 735–742.

17 Alice Marples, 'Scientific Administration in the Early Eighteenth Century: Reinterpreting the Royal Society's Repository,' *Historical Research* (forthcoming, 2018).

18 T. Christopher Bond, 'Keeping Up with the Latest Transactions: The Literary Critique of Scientific Writing in the Hans Sloane Years,' *Eighteenth-Century Life*, 22.2 (1998), 1–7; Thomas Broman, 'Periodical Literature,' in *Books and the Sciences in History*, ed. by Marina Frasca-Spada and Nick Jardine (Cambridge: Cambridge University Press, 2000); Markman Ellis, 'Thomas Birch's "Weekly Letter" (1741–66): Correspondence and History in the Mid-Eighteenth Century Royal Society,' *Notes and Records of the Royal Society of London*, 68.3 (2014),

261–278; Noah Moxham, 'Fit for Print: Developing an Institutional Model of Scientific Periodical Publishing in England, 1665–ca.1714,' *Notes and Records of the Royal Society*, 69 (2015), 241–260.

19 Quoted in Henry Lyons, *The Royal Society 1660–1940* (Cambridge: Cambridge University Press, 1944), p. 107 (italics mine).

20 Hans Sloane, 'The Preface', *Philosophical Transactions* (No. 259) (December 1699), f. *R r r 2.

21 David Spafadora, *The Idea of Progress in Eighteenth-Century Britain* (New Haven: Yale University Press, 1990); Thomas Corns and James Alan Dowie, eds., *Telling the People What to Think: Early Eighteenth Century Periodicals from the Review to the Rambler* (London: Frank Cass, 1993); Helen Berry, 'An Early Coffee House Periodical and Its Readers: The Athenian Mercury, 1691–1697,' *The London Journal*, 25.1 (2000), 14–33; Natasha Glaisyer, 'Readers, Correspondents and Communities: John Houghton's a Collection for the Improvement of Husbandry and Trade (1692–1703),' in *Communities in Early Modern England: Networks, Place, Rhetoric*, ed. by Alexandra Shepard and Phil Withington (Manchester: Manchester University Press, 2000); Brian Cowan, 'Mr. Spectator and the Coffeehouse Public Sphere,' *Eighteenth-Century Studies*, 37.3 (2004), 345–366; Alexander Murdoch, 'A Crucible for Change: Enlightenment in Britain,' in *The Enlightenment World*, ed. by Martin Fitzpatrick et al. (London: Routledge, 2007); Andrew Pettegree, *The Invention of News: How the World Came to Know Itself* (New Haven: Yale University Press, 2014).

22 Carol Gibson-Wood, 'Classification and Value in a Seventeenth-Century Museum: William Courten's Collection,' *Journal of the History of Collections*, 9.1 (1997), 64.

23 London, BL, Sloane MS 4046, f. 170: Thomas Hearne to Hans Sloane (1 January 1721, Edmund Hall, Oxford).

24 London, BL, Sloane MS 4038, f.236: Edward Lhwyd to Hans Sloane (15 September 1701, Oxford).

25 Daniel Margócsy, *Commercial Visions: Science, Trade, and Visual Culture in the Dutch Golden Age* (Chicago: University of Chicago Press, 2015), p. 158.

26 Gibson-Wood, 'Classification and Value', 64.

27 London, BL, Sloane MS 4039, f. 2: James Sutherland to Hans Sloane (7 July 1702, Edinburgh); Sloane MS 4039, f. 157: John Lely to Hans Sloane (2 July 1703, Kew).

28 London, BL, Sloane MS 4038, f. 337: Charles Preston to Hans Sloane (2 May 1702, Edinburgh).

29 Peter S. Morrish, 'Ralph Thoresby (1658–1725) of Leeds, Books and Libraries,' *Library History*, 20.2 (2004), 91.

30 *Ibid.*, 92.

31 D. P. Connell and M. J. Boyd, 'Material from the "Musaeum" of Ralph Thoresby (1658–1725) Preserved at Burton Constable Hall, East Yorkshire,' *Journal of the History of Collections*, 10.1 (1998), 31–40.

32 Paul Potter, 'Taste Sets the Price: Mead, Askew and the Birth of Bibliomania in Eighteenth-Century England,' *Canadian Bulletin of Medical History/Bulletin Canadien d'Histoire de la Médecine*, 12.1 (1995), 241–257; Robin Myers, Michael Harris and Giles Mandelbrote, eds., *Under the Hammer: Book Auctions Since the Seventeenth Century* (London: British Library, 2001); J. E. Elliot, 'The Cost of Reading in Eighteenth-Century Britain: Auction Sale Catalogues and the Cheap Literature Hypothesis,' *ELH*, 77.2 (2010), 353–384.

33 London, BL, Sloane MS 4037, f. 123: William Sherard to Hans Sloane (20 September 1698, Rome).
34 London, BL, Sloane MS 4037, f. 194: Thomas Godwin to Hans Sloane (30 January 1699, Pinner, London).
35 London, BL, Sloane MS 4037, f. 175: Robert Sibbald to Hans Sloane (29 December 1698, Edinburgh); Sloane MS 4037, f. 272: Charles Preston to Hans Sloane (25 May 1699, Edinburgh).
36 London, BL, Sloane MS 4042, f. 142: John Macky to Hans Sloane (10 June 1710, Bruges).
37 London, BL, Sloane MS 4041, f. 2: Archibald Adams to Hans Sloane (30 July 1707, Norwich).
38 Stanley A. Hawkins, 'Sir Hans Sloane (1660–1735): His Life and Legacy,' *The Ulster Medical Journal*, 79.1 (2010), 25.
39 Constance Classen and David Howes, 'The Museum as Sensescape: Western Sensibilities and Indigenous Artefacts,' in *Sensible Objects: Colonialism, Museums and Material Culture*, ed. by Elizabeth Edwards, Chris Godsen and Ruth Philips (Oxford: Berg, 2006).
40 Deborah Harkness, *The Jewell House: Elizabethan London and the Scientific Revolution* (New Haven: Yale University Press, 2007).
41 Kathleen Wilson, 'Citizenship, Empire and Modernity in the English Provinces, c.1720–1790,' *Eighteenth-Century Studies*, 29.1 (1995), 69–96; Colin Kidd, *British Identities before Nationalism: Ethnicity and Nationhood in the Atlantic World 1600–1800* (Cambridge: Cambridge University Press, 1999); Kathleen Wilson, 'The Good, the Bad, and the Impotent: Imperialism and the Politics of Identity in Georgian England,' in *The Consumption of Culture 1600–1800: Image, Object, Text*, ed. by Ann Bermingham and John Brewer (London: Routledge, 2004); Jan Golinski, *British Weather and the Climate of Enlightenment* (Chicago: University of Chicago Press, 2004); Kate Bennett, 'John Aubrey, Hint-Keeper: Life-Writing and the Encouragement of Natural Philosophy in the Pre-Newtonian Seventeenth Century,' *The Seventeenth Century*, 22.2 (2007), 358–380; Vittoria Feola, 'Elias Ashmole's Collections and Views about John Dee,' *Studies in History and Philosophy of Science, Part A*, 43.3 (2012), 530–538; Wolfram Schmidgen, *Exquisite Mixture: The Virtues of Impurity in Early Modern England* (Philadelphia: University of Philadelphia Press, 2013); André Holenstein, Hubert Steinke and Martin Stuber, eds., *Scholars in Action: The Practice of Knowledge and the Figure of the Savant in the 18th Century* (Leiden: Brill, 2013); Elizabeth Yale, *Sociable Knowledge: Natural History and the Nation in Early Modern Britain* (Philadelphia: University of Philadelphia Press, 2016).
42 Bridget Cherry, 'Edward Hatton's New View of London,' *Architectural History*, 44 (2001), 96–105.
43 London, BL, Sloane MS 4059, f. 142: Nicola Francesco Haym to Hans Sloane (undated).
44 *Weekly Journal or Saturday's Post*, Issue 239 (London, England): Saturday 25 May 1723.
45 London, BL, Sloane MS 4042, f. 92: Robert Hales to Hans Sloane (24 January 1709, St James Place).
46 London, BL, Sloane MS 4042, f. 164: Robert Hales to Hans Sloane (3 November 1718, Council Office).
47 P. C. D. Brears, 'Ralph Thoresby, a Museum Visitor in Stuart England,' *Journal of the History of Collections*, 1.2 (1989), 221.

48 *Ibid.*
49 Stephen Botein, Jack R. Censer and Harriet Ritvo, 'The Periodical Press in English and French Society: A Cross-Cultural Approach,' *Comparative Studies in Society and History*, 23.3 (1981), 464–490; Linda Colley, 'Britishness and Otherness: An Argument,' *The Journal of British Studies*, 31.4 (1992), 309–329; Michèle Cohen, *Fashioning Masculinity: National Identity and Language in the Eighteenth Century* (London: Routledge, 1996); Krishnan Kumar, 'English and French National Identity: Comparisons and Contrasts,' *Nations and Nationalism*, 12.3 (2006), 413–432.
50 Birch, *Memoirs* (italics mine); Pulteney, *Historical and Biographical Sketches*, p. 65.
51 Tony Claydon and Ian McBride, eds., *Protestantism and National Identity: Britain and Ireland, c.1650–c.1850* (Cambridge: Cambridge University Press, 1998).
52 *Ibid.*
53 See the chapter by Toby Burrows in this volume.
54 Among the collectors covered in this volume, Sarah Sophia Banks's collection of visiting cards was donated to the British Museum (see the chapter by Arlene Leis in this volume), Morgan and Beatty established their own collections (see the chapter by Laura Cleaver and Danielle Magnusson), and R. E. Hart donated his collection to the Blackburn Public Library (see the chapter by Cynthia Johnston).

3 Sarah Sophia Banks

A 'truly interesting collection of visiting cards and Co.'

Arlene Leis

The British Museum's Trustees Report dated 12 February 1819 notes that John Thomas Smith, the Keeper of Prints and Drawings, was preparing a 'catalogue of Miss Banks's truly interesting collection of visiting cards and Co.'[1] The collection to which the report refers is that of Sarah Sophia Banks (1744–1818), sister of the well-known botanist, collector and President of the Royal Society Sir Joseph Banks. Sarah Sophia's status as the sibling of an eminent public figure has detracted attention from the critical attention her work has received during the two centuries since her death. However, as this chapter will demonstrate, Sarah Sophia was an active collector in her own right, and to regard her projects as mere offshoots of her brother's ventures would be to grossly underestimate their independent importance. At the time of her death, her stockpile of paper items boasted well over 19,000 articles; now housed at the British Museum and British Library, it comprises admission tickets, playbills, fashion plates, political caricatures, satirical prints, ballads, political prints, watch plates, trade cards, newspaper clippings, bookplates and visitor cards, amongst other items.[2] Sarah Sophia also collected coins and medals: over 9,000 specimens are divided between the British Museum and Royal Mint.[3]

Today, within the museum environment, some parts of Sarah Sophia's print collection have been disassembled, recatalogued and combined with other collections; however, certain key elements remain intact, and these provide clues to her collecting methodologies. First, there survives in the British Museum a substantial number of the mounts she created for systematizing and displaying smaller items like admission tickets, visiting tickets and bookplates. There are also some albums of satirical prints that have been maintained as originally assembled. Importantly, the British Library holds a manuscript catalogue naming the 'books, etc.' that were situated in the domestic quarters of the Banks residence at 32 Soho Square.[4] In this inventory, which contains c. 300 pages and measures 31.4 cm x 19.8 cm, she lists all her printed collections and describes how they were organized within different rooms and compartments of the house.[5] Today it is an essential complement to another library inventory produced by H. H. Baber and H. F. Cary in 1820–1823, which records the contents and location of items in Sir Joseph's library. This document is particularly useful when studying the collection today because, unlike auction catalogues, which briefly list items in lots, the inventory provides detailed information about the arrangement and methodology of the existing collection.

During Sarah Sophia's life, her large collection was stored alongside her brother's herbarium, library and printing press in the house that she lived in with Sir Joseph at 32 Soho Square, London, a thriving scientific hub where natural history specimens were collected, studied and exchanged.

Focusing predominantly on Sarah Sophia's collection of printed materials alongside the aforementioned inventory, this chapter will explore Sarah Sophia's complex and innovative collecting practices and methodologies. Importantly, it will consider the collections of the Banks siblings as meaningfully interconnected but also distinct, reclaiming Sarah Sophia's place in the house as an authoritative collector and 'curator.' In doing so, it will demonstrate that women participated in and helped shape scientific and cultural pursuits in ways often undocumented by traditional narratives of the eighteenth century.

Sister and collector

There is no record of who or what inspired Sarah Sophia's collecting, but the siblings shared an early passion for acquisition. As a boy, Joseph began assembling a collection of plants, flowers, shells, stones, insects, animals, fish and fossils from the natural surroundings at Revesby Abby, the Banks's family seat located in Lincolnshire.[6] Sarah Sophia may have assisted him, as she appears to have been collecting paper items at that time. One of her visiting tickets – a card belonging to the Duchess of Northumberland – is annotated with a date of 1754. If this annotation indicates the year of acquisition, as notes on other items do, then it suggests that Sarah Sophia had begun collecting printed materials by the age of 10. Sir Joseph later claimed his mother, who lent him her copy of Gerard's *Herball*, inspired his early collecting, but Sarah Sophia seems to have followed her father and grandfather's antiquarian pursuits. Both father and grandfather were members of the Society of Antiquarians of London and the Spalding Gentleman's Society, a Lincolnshire club formed in 1710 that met and discussed local antiquities.[7] This might explain Sarah Sophia's zeal for gathering heraldic, topographical and antiquarian literature – all genres that are well represented in her collection.

The co-collecting Bankses remained close throughout their adult lives. Indeed, contextual evidence suggests that Nathaniel Hone's miniature portrait of Sarah Sophia, dating from 1768, may have been a token of affection for her brother (see Figure 3.1). Hone's portrait – a conventional head-and-shoulders

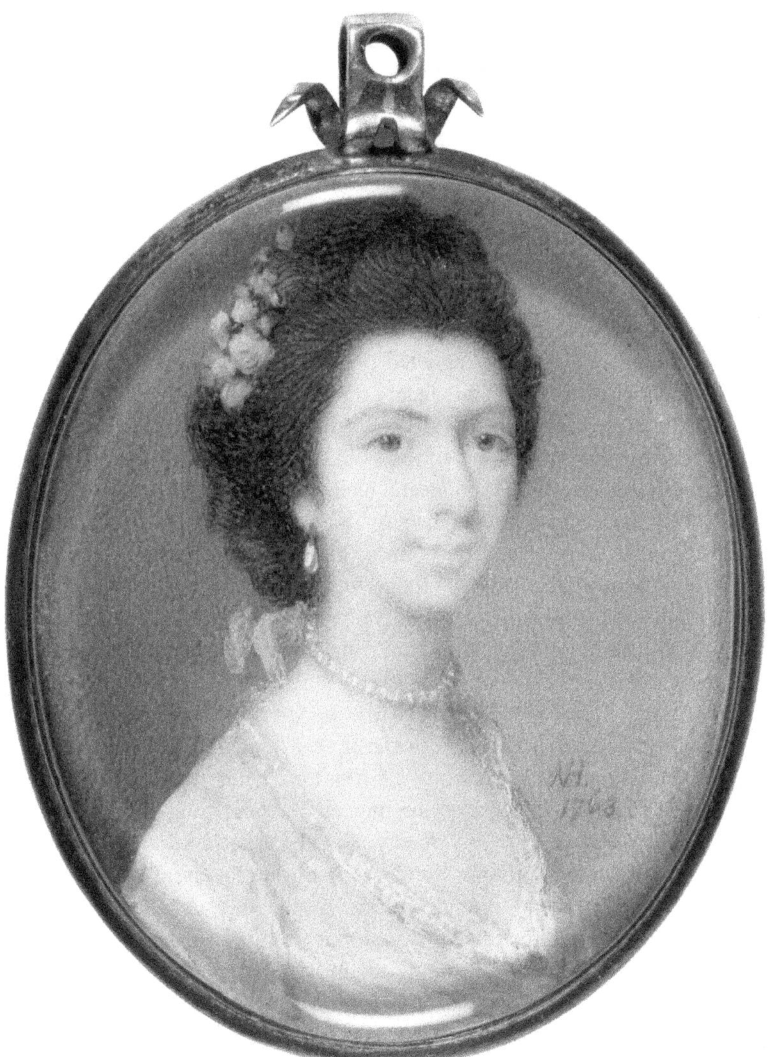

Figure 3.1 Nathaniel Hone the Elder, Irish, 1718–1784, *Sarah Sophia Banks* (1768, watercolour on ivory, 4.5 x 3.8 cm)

National Gallery of Ireland NGI.2717 (Photo © National Gallery of Ireland)

view – depicts Sarah Sophia at 24 years of age. Since her brother was to depart with James Cook on his first South Pacific voyage the same year in which the portrait was created, it is possible that Sarah Sophia presented this token of tenderness to him before his departure. Hone has delicately rendered her facial features and emphasized her girlish femininity by showing her in a pale, pink dress trimmed with dainty lace. She wears pearl drop earrings and a matching pearl necklace that is tied with a pink ribbon at the back of her neck. Tiny pink roses decorate her hair. The portrait miniature is the most intimate of all portraits. Its small size makes it easy to transport; one can carry it close to one's body at all times. Accordingly, portrait miniatures were often commissioned to alleviate the pains of absence.

Their close relationship enabled Sarah Sophia to create strategically a supporting role for herself in her brother's career. When Sir Joseph returned from the *Endeavour* voyage with Cook, he immediately began pursuing an intense form of self-promotion and scientific dissemination. He hired the fashionable artists Sir Joshua Reynolds and Benjamin West to paint his portrait. These images were reproduced as engraved pictures for easy circulation across a broader public sphere. He immediately rented a home at 14 New Burlington Street in London where he kept the objects he had collected abroad and transformed the building into a kind of museum of the South Seas. At the front of the house were three public rooms at which various natural and artificial curiosities from the voyage were on display.[8] Sarah Sophia's collection includes a visitor ticket with her name on it from this London address. She probably lived there too and assisted her brother with organizing and storing the collection and with receiving visitors and giving tours.

By 1777, the collections at 14 New Burlington had grown sufficiently as to require additional space, so Sir Joseph purchased a terraced home at 32 Soho Square. Sarah Sophia noticed the opportunity to set up household with her brother and wrote to him, offering her own money to help him purchase the house – or at least to buy the furniture. Upon receiving his refusal, she wrote that he was only indulging himself and not letting her 'have a little share of the pleasure' of his company, and she asked him to, 'humour her and grant her request.'[9] Sarah Sophia is likely to have realized that living with her brother would provide access to the various social circles in which he moved, presenting an opportunity for her to carve a niche for herself as a collector in semi-public realms. Sir Joseph however was busy renovating various rooms of the house, and he added an extensive library, printing room and herbarium to the back of the building. This additional section became a type of scientific laboratory, and turned 32 Soho Square into a well-known centre for scientific activities. Sir Joseph hired a principal curator, the Swedish botanist Dr. Daniel Solander, as well as numerous other colleagues to help supervise his plethora of natural specimens. One year after his purchase of 32 Soho Square, the 36-year-old Joseph wed the 20-year-old heiress Dorothea Hugessen. Two years later, in 1780, once Joseph and Dorothea were settled, they invited Sarah Sophia to live with them, and she resided with them permanently thereafter.

The trio of Bankses shared a busy social calendar, which is evident in the admission tickets, invitations and visiting tickets Sarah Sophia collected. For example they attended numerous breakfast and dinner parties, went to theatres and lectures, visited homes like Horace Walpole's Strawberry Hill and attended trials, such as that of Warren Hastings. Such artefacts confirm that living with Sir Joseph and Lady Banks enabled Sarah Sophia to continue the intellectual and social pursuits she enjoyed and to live a single life without the social ostracism customarily experienced by women who wished to continue studies after youth.

Modes of acquisition

According to the dates annotating objects in Sarah Sophia's collection, her collection grew substantially when she moved into Soho Square. It is also during this time that the siblings' collecting practices reflect overlapping interests and influences. Most notably, the collections exhibit a mutual fascination with 'ephemera.' An art historical definition of ephemera evokes paper objects intended to last temporarily. Indeed, the term 'ephemera' stems from the Greek term *ephemerides*, meaning diary or calendar; traditionally ephemera were objects associated with the passing of time.[10] Revealingly, the *Oxford English Dictionary* notes that the term can also refer to organisms found in nature whose lifespan is one day, such as the mayfly insect. Not only do both collections evoke the ephemeral; they also undermine it. The continuing preservation of their collections for future generations not only blurs the line between the natural and artificial, it challenges viewers to reconceptualize notions of time.

One way in which Sarah Sophia benefitted from her proximity to Sir Joseph was through his social networks. Evidence in the form of letters demonstrates that her brother's national and international acquaintances and employees were well aware of his sister's collections; indeed, they contributed to them frequently.[11] For example, on 21 October 1797, Johann Friedrich Blumenbach, often considered the father of physical anthropology, offered numismatic papers for Miss Banks along with pamphlets and a card (visitor card) of the widow Guinhard, 'the favorite of Frederick of Prussia.'[12] Numerous letters addressed to her brother and some of the notes she made next to items in the collection prove that she had a remarkable flow of gifts coming from colonial contacts, as well as national and international clergy, artists, diplomats, naturalists and travellers.

Although Sarah Sophia clearly capitalized on her brother's cosmopolitan network, various visiting cards, fashion plates and admission tickets from her collection feature annotations that reveal she also exchanged items through her own connections, which included networks of other women. One letter accompanying some admission tickets in her collection reveals that a Mrs. J. Wheler had sent them to her.[13] In one letter to Sir Joseph from the entrepreneur and owner of the Birmingham Soho Mint, Mathew Boulton, Boulton thanks Sarah Sophia for passing 'some of his dollars to the Princesses.'[14] Importantly, Lady Dorothea Banks's contribution should not be overlooked; she too would have clipped newspaper articles of interest or trade cards for Sarah Sophia and some admission tickets and visitor cards in the collection bear her name on them.

Sarah Sophia also obtained artefacts through her own diligent searching. Accompanied by a 'servant,' she sometimes travelled around London in the hope of finding pieces for her collections.[15] Surely she visited book dealers, print sellers and engravers and these are well represented in her collection of trade cards. But given the variety of her collection, she is likely to have tapped less conventional sources, too. One can imagine her passing by a coffee house to have a quick rummage through a pile of newspapers.

Sarah Sophia was a dynamic collector who deployed a wide variety of methods for gathering up the material culture she sought. Her collection suggests a fascination with the local and the global. Having reviewed some of the means with which she built up her collection, we can now turn to its contents.

Preservation of items: common methods

In their methodology, organization and storage, Sarah Sophia's collections complemented those of her brother. Both Bankses sought to preserve ephemeral objects and associated data for long-term study, and the storage of fragile specimens necessitates specialized archival paraphernalia: mounts, labels, folders, storage boxes, ink and adhesives. Both siblings made use of all these tools. They both pressed their artefacts carefully then mounted them onto stiff, white paper. Both accompanied each item with essential data, such as the date of receipt, a physical description, and an indication of geographical provenance. Both made use of new methods for the organizing of specimen sheets, too. Prior to the late eighteenth century, it was standard practice for both natural history and print collectors to bind these sheets into books. However, Sir Joseph and Dr. Solander introduced to Britain the new method of organization that the Swedish botanist Carl Linnaeus devised; that is, they maintained the plant collections on folded free mounts instead of binding them into books. Specimen sheets were then stacked into groups by category. Leaving them unbound made it convenient for collectors to add to the collection and easily re-order the mounts within cabinets. Both Sir Joseph and Sarah Sophia adopted this practice, Sir Joseph for his collection of dry plants and Sarah Sophia for her collections of smaller paper items, such as admission tickets, visiting tickets, and bookplates.

Both collections were stored in boxes, cabinets and Solander cases. A Solander case was a special hardcover archival box used for storing natural history specimens. It was invented by Dr. Solander while he was cataloguing the natural history collections at Soho Square and the British Museum. Sarah Sophia appears to have helped pioneer this storage method for paper items; bibliographical societies began recommending Solander cases for the preservation of wrappers, boards and cloth materials right around the time Sarah Sophia began using them for this purpose. They subsequently became well established as a means of storage for books, manuscripts and prints.

Another similarity between the two collections is that Sir Joseph and Sarah Sophia both aspired to the possession of ‘types,’ that is, the original specimens on which the study of a species is founded. Sir Joseph collected and documented botanical ‘types’ in his herbarium. Sarah Sophia, similarly, acquired first editions, series, new editions and/or samples of engraving, thereby exploring any given ‘species’ in all of its forms.

Sniping, sorting and sticking

There are many overlapping similarities between Sarah Sophia’s collecting practices and those of her brother; however, she also customized her brother’s natural history methods to her own ends. Importantly, Sarah Sophia’s collecting practices also resonate with broader trends in eighteenth-century collecting and graphic culture. First of all, her collection is divided according to category of object and the practical dictates of scale. According to her inventory of items, substantial sized prints and broadsheets were usually catalogued and bound into large portfolios of various dimensions.[16] To fill her portfolios, she regularly purchased prints. Next to the prints, she writes useful annotations, such as the year of acquisition and/or the names of persons depicted, as exemplified in this page from a portfolio holding numerous political caricatures by the English engraver James Sayers (see Figure 3.2). The substantial sized album contains numerous prints she collected, including Sayers’s series of small, full-length public figures of the day and political cartoons like *Mr. Burke’s Fair of Spectacles for short sighted Politicians*. Here Sarah Sophia numbers the figures at the bottom of the print and creates a key on the opposite page that identifies who’s

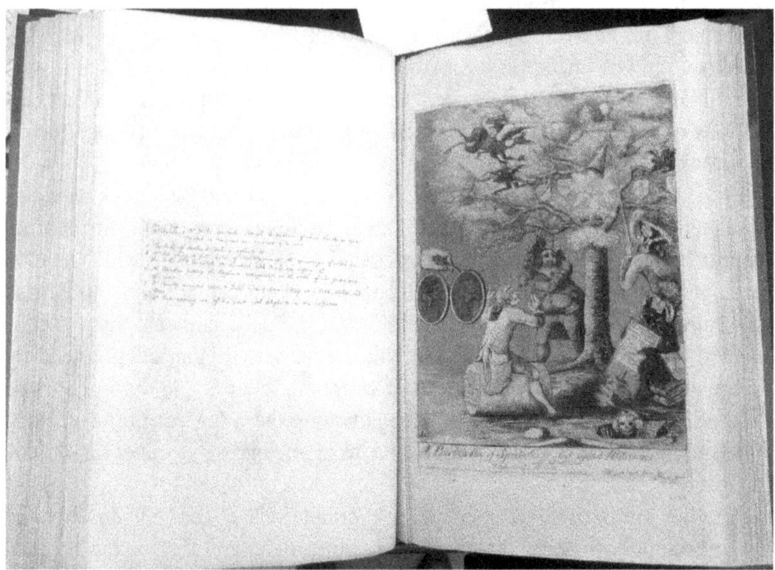

Figure 3.2 James Sayers, *Mr. Burke's pair of spectacles for short-sighted politicians*, etching and aquatint, published 12 May 1791

Collection of Sarah Sophia Banks, British Museum, Y,10.128 (© The Trustees of the British Museum)

who in the picture, and she writes a brief explanation of what takes place in the picture. Today, this album of originals is particularly useful when comparing later reproductions of the same works.

The smaller items she collected – trade cards, admission tickets, book tickets, visitor tickets, newspaper snippets, watch plates, among other items – were glued with wet adhesives onto sheets of paper measuring 18 ¼ x 23 ½ inches. These large sheets of white paper were folded vertically to create lightweight folders, the contents of which were recorded in pen on the outside. Next to each item in the folder she often writes in ink the year she received it; as a result, her arrangement disregards the chronological sequence of the events depicted and the history of the collections takes precedence.

Although some academics in the past have accused Sarah Sophia of 'hoarding,' the practice of collecting enabled Sarah Sophia to create a wide range of inventive classifications and arrangements. As mentioned previously, she was influenced by the Linnaean methodology her brother utilized for organizing his natural history specimens, but she also devised her own classificatory systems, creating taxonomies that best suited the material she collected. According to her hand-labeled mounts, she simultaneously categorized her collection of visiting tickets based on social hierarchies, aesthetic features and geographical origins. Interestingly, each method of systematization invites viewers to contemplate the same type of object in a different way.

First, drawing on Linnaean taxonomy, she adopts a hierarchical system of classification, organizing tickets according to the social status of the people they represent. Her mounts of nobility are organized by rank, from 'English Dukes' down to 'Irish Peers' and 'British Persons' to 'Irish Persons.' These categories of cards are pasted into columns and family groups reminiscent of a family tree (see Figure 3.3). The left-hand columns are almost always complete and follow on from one another. The right-hand columns are often slotted at a later date, suggesting that she was constantly adding to the collection. These later additions might showcase a new card design, or someone's new address, title and/or marital status and as such she kept her collection up to date by tracking social changes over time.

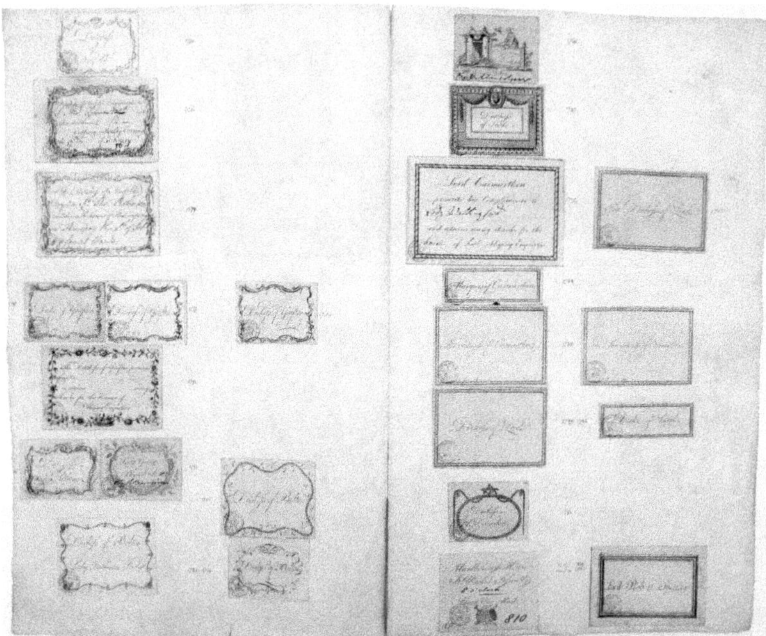

Figure 3.3 Mount of visiting cards 'Dukes,' collection of Sarah Sophia Banks, British Museum, C,1.1–24

In contrast to the focus on British Titled Persons, Peers and Persons, Sarah Sophia then goes on to group together her 'Blanks' visiting tickets. These are visitor tickets usually without names: samples taken mostly from engraver's books. 'Blanks' are grouped together alphabetically, according to their stylistic characteristics or subject, highlighting their use of 'squares,' 'garlands,' 'figures,' 'architecture,' 'dogs,' 'gondolas,' 'flowers' and so on (see Figure 3.4). In these volumes of blanks, the designs and engravers of the cards take precedence over their holders or their country of origin. They show Sarah Sophia's desire to collect for decorative value and for their look upon the page. Her organization encouraged viewers to compare and contrast cards on a different basis than simply social rank.

Next, visitor tickets classified under her 'foreign' designation, deriving from the continent and as far away as China and America, are organized alphabetically by the country in which they were produced and circulated, encouraging international comparison (see Figure 3.5). These cards also display the names of persons of rank, but they are not arranged accordingly;

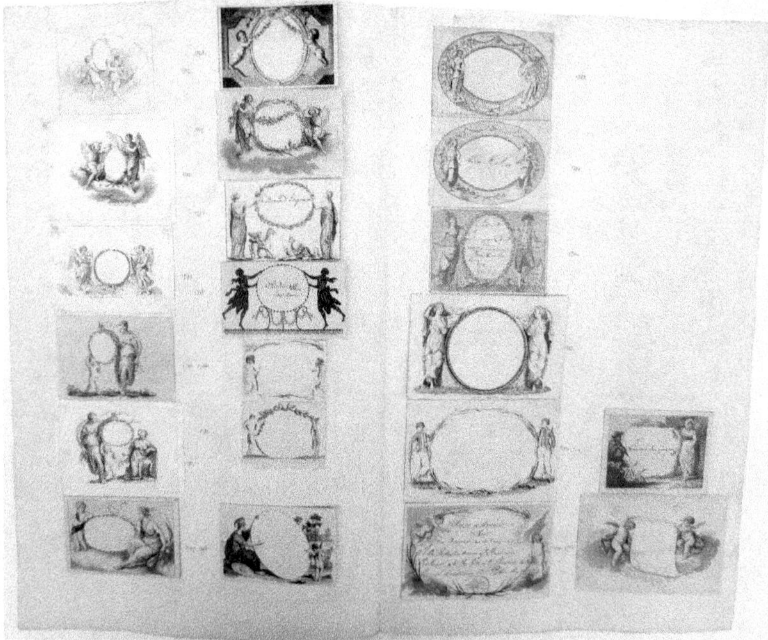

Figure 3.4 Mount of visiting cards 'Figures,' collection of Sarah Sophia Banks, British Museum, C,1.2550–2570

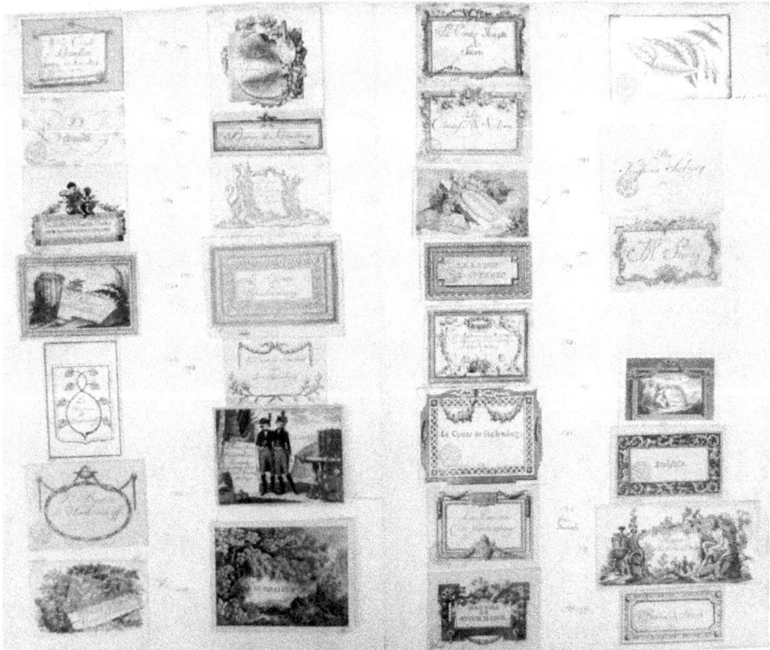

Figure 3.5 Mount of visiting cards 'Germany,' collection of Sarah Sophia Banks, British Museum, D,1.535–566

they are simply pasted in rows. Sarah Sophia includes more annotations next to the images on these cards, and often they represent monuments or landscapes specific to those areas. She also provides contextual information about a card's symbolic history. The cosmopolitan flavour of her collection of visitor tickets suggest a fascination with the global, and while she never travelled abroad like her brother, Sarah Sophia could travel by way of her visitor tickets.

Sarah Sophia's collection of over 4,000 national and international admission tickets on to mounts further emphasizes the organizational methods she explored. She usually organized them according to venue or specific type of event, such as 'Haymarket Theatre' or 'Balloons.' Comparing her admission ticket mounts, she appears to have glued paper objects on the page as she collected; this is seen in the mounts displaying admission tickets for 'Concerts (Bach's)' and another for 'Plays' (see Figures 3.6 and 3.7). The Bach concert tickets are kept as part of a series with a notice explaining how and where to obtain tickets; such inserts provide a

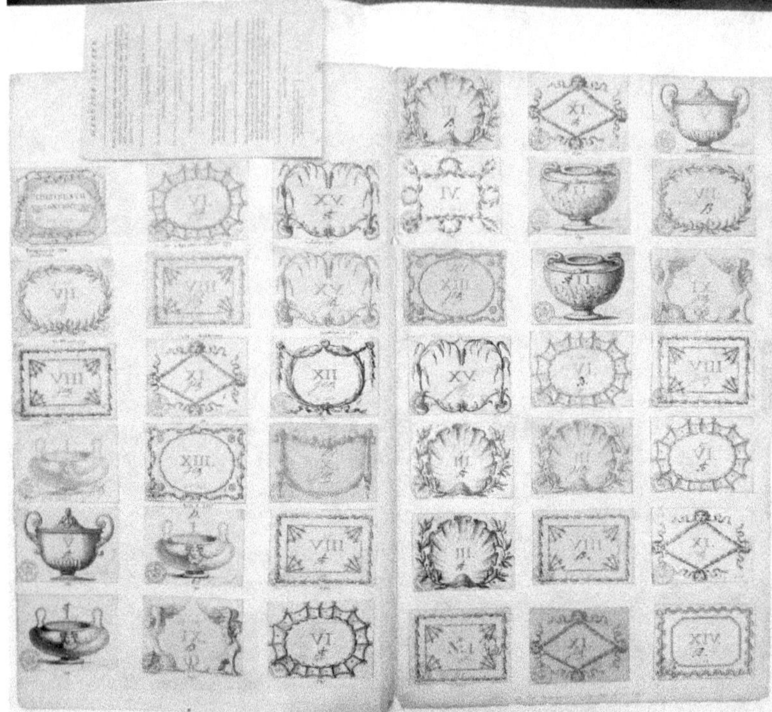

Figure 3.6 Mount of admission tickets 'Concerts (Bach's),' collection of Sarah Sophia Banks, British Museum, J,9.572–611

rich contextual background to the tickets. She glues them in even, straight rows, but they are not pasted sequentially.

In contrast to her 'Concerts (Bach's)' tickets, the 'Plays' tickets are pasted randomly on the mount. This method of chance created an asymmetrical layout of combination and overlap with different-sized works and varied pictures. Sometimes multiples of the same tickets are glued on one mount. Seals are signs of authenticity. Her arrangements often alternate between a rigorous visual order and crowded bricolage, bringing together unexpected visuals and conflicting narratives. They are an expression not only of her own tastes and aesthetic sensibilities but of the tastes of a specific time period of which she was a part. She also adds some contextual information to this mount. Her annotations also provide more details and rectifications. One ticket for Mr. Fawcett's benefit shows a neoclassical building design; next to it she writes 'designed by Wyatt and intended

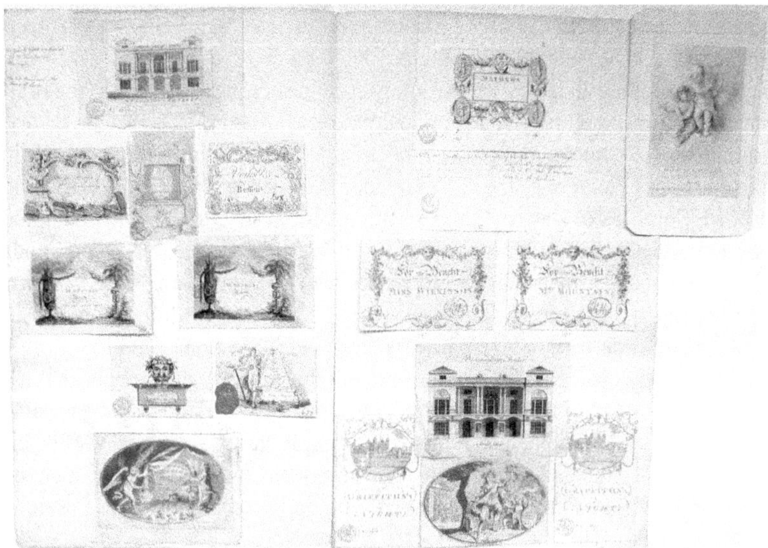

Figure 3.7 Mount of admission tickets 'Plays,' collection of Sarah Sophia Banks, British Museum C,2.1622–1639

for the theatre at Birmingham.' She continues, 'the act thrown out in the House of Lords.' Not only are the images on tickets interesting to engage with as a record of design and printed lettering, but these mounts demonstrate something of the social and cultural history of a specific time. Sarah Sophia was finding new ways to organize, describe and preserve information that could be passed along to future generations.

Sarah Sophia adopted numerous modes for arranging her vast collection of print culture. Snipping, sorting and sticking a broad range of graphic material between sheets of paper not only provided her with a means to store and manage the collection; it enabled her to unite systematic knowledge with aesthetic and social pleasures.

The manuscript inventory: negotiating shared space

As well as sharing many of her brother's preservation methods, Sarah Sophia also shared his domestic area. Her inventory reveals that within the domestic area of Soho Square, she constructed her own collecting spaces in rooms where the domestic and social functions played an important part. According to its detail and the number of printed items it lists, the handwritten catalogue further demonstrates Sarah Sophia's collecting practice as essentially systematic.

Sarah Sophia's handwritten inventory provides further insight into the principles that informed her organizational practices. According to the inventory, Sarah Sophia's books and printed material were stored around six rooms in the domestic quarters: the L(ittle) room or Anteroom, Front Drawing Room, South Room, Mrs. Banks's Room, Room up 3 pr. [pairs] stairs and the Dressing Room.[17] On the top of the first page, she created a letter-code that conveniently maps the exact places where items were stored around the house. In each room, select pieces of furniture – wardrobes, bookcases and a pianoforte case – housed items from her collections. The key further describes how some items were kept: on the ground; in drawers; behind wire doors; in oak, mahogany and deal boxes; on shelves; in cubes (possibly the same type of Chippendale cubes Sir Joseph had made especially for his botanical specimens); in drawers and in Solander cases. The manuscript reveals that Sarah Sophia employed numerous techniques of closeting, staking and shelving her collections.

This catalogue does not record any of her coins, medals or tokens, even though these were also kept at 32 Soho Square; those objects are documented in separate volumes. This reveals that materiality was an important factor when organizing her collections. The manuscript records well over 1,000 books covering a range of subjects, including religion, antiquities, numismatics, novels, heraldry, archery, history, tours, recipes and some museum catalogues. It meticulously names her printed materials, including the titles of her extensive collection of 'musick' sheets (whereabouts now unknown). She also lists all the titles of the satirical prints she owned along with the prices she paid for them. Also recorded is an extensive collection of playbills, which are ordered under comedy, tragedy, comic opera and farce. This collection of theatrical, printed material was stored in cubes at Revesby Abbey, the Banks family's seat in Lincolnshire.

Like the collection itself, the inventory also shows experimentation with diverse modes of classification. Initially, printed materials are listed alphabetically, according to author and title, rather than by genre. When comparing their locations around the house, we see that 'High' forms of print culture, poetry and classical literature, intermingle in the same rooms with 'low' forms, such as magazines and ballads. In subsequent sections of the document, however, she experiments with drawing upon thematic and other methods of organization. The apparent inconsistencies of the inventory are as fascinating as its obvious efficiencies. For example, under 'Visiting Tickets,' which is listed among other categories of items beginning with 'V' in her alphabetical list, Banks includes complex and at times confusing sub-listings. In block entries, with little information, she records under 'Visiting Tickets' the existence of four volumes of 'Admission tickets' and two volumes of 'Shop bills,' as well as a wide range of other ephemera from all over the house. She lists, for instance, numerous portfolios featuring a variety of prints, including one that contained 'predominately trash.' It is uncertain why she chose to classify numerous diverse items under V and more specifically below the collection of 'Visitor cards,' especially since these items were not stored in the same area of the home. It might be because of undocumented material or aesthetic similarities. In any case, the inventory is a useful guide when studying her collections today, and it reveals yet another layer of Sarah Sophia's obsessive preoccupation to organize and arrange, but it also conveys the occasional inadequacy of classificatory systems when seeking to organize a vast array of objects.

Collecting and sociability at 32 Soho Square

Engaging with Sarah Sophia's inventory, albums and mounts offers a glimpse into her creative collecting practices. However, just as important as the process of acquisition and systematization is the way in which visitors appreciated the collection during Sarah Sophia's time. Taking into consideration the position of her collection within the Banks residence at 32 Soho Square, we can now examine some of the ways in which scientific knowledge and sociability were physically intermingled within the Banks's home.

Sarah Sophia's collection was a vehicle for polite sociability, and social events were central to the house's public identity. Sir Joseph's first biographer, Edward Smith, describes 32 Soho Square as 'a vast museum'; while the aforementioned Dr. Solander acted as Sir Joseph's curator and librarian, Sarah Sophia was 'mistress of the house.'[18] F. H. W. Sheppard describes the interior as 'light-filled, with many windows, and magnificently installed with fluted friezes, classically inspired arches and embellished capitals.'[19] According to Harold B. Carter's floor plan of 32 Soho Square, 'Miss Banks's bedroom' and 'dressing room' were located on the first floor, directly across from the 'drawing room' and the 'south room,' also known as the great room. This means that Sarah Sophia occupied the area of the house used for hosting many social events, including regular Sunday soirees in the south room that were attended by both men and women.[20] Unlike the customary letter of introduction needed to enter Sir Joseph's library and herbarium, the gatherings taking place in the domestic area do not seem to have been rigidly planned events with any fixed limit to the number of participants, set guest list or any particular rules. However, a notebook from Soho Square indicates that the Banks family recorded the weights of all the visitors to the house from 1778 sporadically up to 1814.[21] Like her inventory, the notebook further emphasizes Sarah Sophia's concern with organizing, recording and storing. As hostess to the many gatherings taking place in the great room at Soho Square, Sarah Sophia played an important role in helping her brother foster connections for institutions, such as the Royal Society, British Museum and other committees representing the arts and sciences of which her brother supported.

Social events were central to the house's public identity, and in the great room the cementing of bonds was as important as the customary reading of research papers at the more public institutional society meetings. Guests could discuss their projects, ambitions and latest discoveries in the natural sciences and women could offer their perspectives. Visitors to 32 Soho Square commented positively on their time there. The orientalist and vice president of the Royal Society William Marsden wrote that, at the Banks residence, 'one met a variety of persons and acquired information of what was going forward in the world of literature and science.'[22] The Dutch anatomist Pieter Camper wrote enthusiastically about his time visiting 32 Soho Square: 'Nowhere is there to be found a house, a library and company as that of Sir Joseph!'[23] Visitors to 32 Soho Square came to engage with both Sir Joseph's and Sarah Sophia's collections. Visitors could sift through cabinets, flip through albums, read books and touch objects. Those with an interest in coinage, and the graphic and commercial arts more specifically, would seize the opportunity to examine Sarah Sophia's massive collections. Sarah Sophia could showcase her collections and visitors would have been encouraged to partake in a kind of sociable exchange that both merged science and the arts and strengthened interdisciplinary networks.

The logistics of the collections within the house emphasize the interrelationship between the Banks collections, as well as between the arts and sciences; Sarah Sophia's artificialia provided a symbolic counterpart to her brother's collection of naturalia. For example, her much-cherished collections of music, heraldry and some of her visiting cards were kept in the anteroom, which was located next to her brother's study and just between the foyer of the domestic space and Sir Joseph's scientific headquarters at the back of the building; her collection of artificialia thus served as a gateway to Sir Joseph's naturalia. The display of natural and artificial collections draws on the same methodology used for many private cabinets and public institutional collections, such as the British Museum and the Royal Society, that sought to explain the universe through notions of empirical classification of natural and man-made objects. Unsurprisingly, the Banks home at 32 Soho Square was located near the British Museum, of which Sir Joseph was trustee, and not far from Somerset House, home to the Royal Society, of which he was President. A further association between the Banks home at 32 Soho Square and the Royal Society is evident in the large communal park situated in the middle of the square where a statue of Charles II, who signed the first Royal Charter to the Royal Society in 1662, was installed in 1681. Collections like those of the Bankses, the Royal Society and the British Museum, universal in scope and highly taxonomical, reflected an eighteenth-century curiosity toward the world at large and a desire of knowledge for the improvement of mankind. Many of these characteristics were shared with, and derived from, the collections of Sir Hans Sloane, who was also a President of the Royal Society and whose collections were at the foundation of the British Museum.[24] These were values the Banks family promoted.

Conclusion

In November 1818, shortly after Sarah Sophia's death, her sister-in-law, Lady Dorothea Banks, donated parts of the collection to the Royal Mint and British Museum. When the paper collection arrived at the British Museum, it was accepted within 'Antiquities,' a department increasingly acknowledged as being 'a repository of many of the greatest works of European draughtsmanship.'[25] The department already held notable prints and drawings by masters such as Hans Holbein, Peter Paul Rubens and Rembrandt van Rijn. The librarian and antiquarian Sir Henry Ellis assessed her collection's value to be just £150.[26] Importantly, he also noted that the collection provided many examples of 'the first efforts of our Celebrated Engravers.'[27] Indeed, her collection contains a plethora of large- and small-scale examples from national and international artists, anonymous works and some produced by lesser-known artists. Despite the modest financial value, the Museum acknowledged her paper collection for its scope and artistic value, and the fact that it was assembled by a woman may have rendered it all the more fascinating because most of the collections accepted by the Museum at that time were assembled by men.

The Museum's fascination with Sarah Sophia's 'truly interesting collection' is unsurprising; characterized by its breath and variety, collections of these types are scarce. The bestowal of this enormous body of graphic material to this particular institution not only secured its permanence, it meant that the items collected by Sarah Sophia could be made available to a far wider public that had been the case during her lifetime.

Today, the paper collection survives predominantly in the British Museum's Department of Prints, but nine albums of assorted items, along with her collections of books and playbills, were later transferred to the British Library. Her paper and coin collections have been digitized to high standards and added to the British Museum's digital image archive (Merlin) where they are easily searchable. Her collection is recognized as part of the

British Museum's foundational collections, and she is commemorated in a display dedicated to her in the Museum's 'Collecting the World' gallery.

Printed materials were an endless fascination for Sarah Sophia. The fact that her paper collection outlived its collector renders it all the more rare. In its arrangement, display and storage at 32 Soho Square, it blurred the boundaries of science and art and attested to the centrality of visual culture within the world of polite science. Amassing and cataloguing the collection took decades. Her collections of printed material, which she built during the eighteenth and early nineteenth centuries, are dominated mostly by national and international types of specimens produced by engravers of this period. They might also be said to illustrate the contemporary impulse to preserve ephemeral material for posterity, which can also be seen at work in the collections of Hans Sloane and Thomas Phillipps.[28]

Today, the collection of Sarah Sophia Banks can be viewed as a working reference collection that conveys her engagement with society and the commercial texts and aesthetics of a wider print culture. As a working repository, it is useful in many related disciplines, such as history, art history and sociology.

Notes

1 British Museum, *Central Archive Trustees Reports*, vol. 1 (London: British Museum, 1811–1840).

2 Antony Griffiths, *The Department of Prints and Drawings in the British Museum: User's Guide* (London: British Museum, 1987), pp. 82–84. The collection at the British Library can be found as Sarah Sophia Banks, A Collection of Broadsides, Cuttings from Newspapers, Engravings, etc. of Various Dates, Formed by Miss S. S. Banks, 9 vols L. R. 301.h.3–11. British Library, London. For research on her paper collections see: Anthony Pincott, 'The Book Tickets of Miss Sarah Sophia Banks (1744–1818),' *The Bookplate Journal*, 2.1 (2004), 3–30; Arlene Leis, 'Displaying Art and Fashion: Ladies' Pocket-Book Imagery in the Paper Collections of Sarah Sophia Banks,' *Konsthistorisk tidskrift/Journal of Art History* (2013), 252–271; Arlene Leis, 'Cutting, Arranging and Pasting: Sarah Sophia Banks as Collector,' *Early Modern Women: An Interdisciplinary Journal*, 9.1 (2014), 127–140; Arlene Leis, 'Ephemeral Histories: Social Commemoration of the Revolutionary and Napoleonic Wars in the Paper Collections of Sarah Sophia Banks,' in *Visual Culture and the Revolutionary and Napoleonic Wars*, ed. by Satish Padiyar, Philip Shaw and Philippa Simpson (London and New York: Routledge, 2017), pp. 183–199.

3 For research on her coins and medals see: Catherine Eagleton, 'Collecting African Money in Georgian London: Sarah Sophia Banks and Her Collection of Coins,' *Museum History Journal*, 6.1 (2013), 23–24; R. J. Eaglen, 'Sarah Sophia Banks and Her English Hammered Coins,' *British Numismatic Society,*

78 (2008), 200–215; Catherine Eagleton, 'Collecting America: Sarah Sophia Banks and the "Continental Dollar" of 1776,' *The Numismatic Chronicle*, 174 (2014), 293–301

4 Sarah Sophia Banks, *A Manuscript Catalogue of the Library and Collection of Prints Belonging to Sir Joseph Banks*, London, British Library, 460.d.13.
5 *Ibid.*
6 Harold B. Carter, *Sir Joseph Banks* (London: British Museum, 1988), p. 24.
7 William Moore, *The Gentlemen's Society at Spalding: Its Origin and Progress* (London: William Pickering, 1851), p. 23.
8 Neil Chambers, *Joseph Banks and the British Museum* (London: Pickering and Chatto, 2007), p. 9.
9 Carter, *Sir Joseph Banks*, p. 153; John Gascoigne, *Joseph Banks and the English Enlightenment: Useful Knowledge and Polite Culture* (Cambridge: University Press, 1994), p. 24.
10 Alan Clinton, *Printed Ephemera: Collection, Organization and Access* (London: Clive Bingley, 1981), pp. 15–21.
11 William Dawson, *The Banks Letters: A Calendar of the Manuscript Correspondence of Sir Joseph Banks Preserved in the British Museum/The British Museum (Natural History) and Other Collections in Great Britain*, ed. by William Dawson (London: British Museum, 1958), pp. 115, 121, 139, 141, 305, 389.
12 Dawson, *The Banks Letters*, p. 115.
13 Sarah Sophia Banks Collection, British Museum, Prints and Drawings, J. 9–171–189.
14 Dawson, *The Banks Letters*, pp. 139, 141.
15 Thomas Smith, *A Book for a Rainy Day or Recollections of the Events of the Years 1766–1833* (London: Methuen & Co., 1845), p. 141.
16 Sarah Sophia Banks, *A Catalogue of Books*, British Library, 460.d. 13. For more on the eighteenth-century practice of print collecting, see for example: John Brewer, *The Pleasures of the Imagination: English Culture in the Eighteenth Century* (London: HarperCollins, 1997), pp. 450–456; Timothy Clayton, *The English Print 1688–1802* (New Haven and London: Yale University Press, 1997); Lucy Peltz, *Facing the Text: Extra-Illustration, Print Culture and Society in Britain 1769–1840* (San Marino, CA: Huntington Library Press, 2017).
17 Sarah Sophia Banks, *A Catalogue of Books*, British Library, 460.d.13.
18 Edward Smith, *The Life of Sir Joseph Banks* (Honolulu: University Press of the Pacific, 2002), pp. 62–63.
19 F. H. W. Sheppard, 'Soho Square Area: Portland Estate: Nos 31–32 Soho Square: Twentieth Century House,' *Survey of London: Volumes 33 and 34: St. Anne Soho* (1966), www.british-history.ac.uk/report.aspx?compid=41059 (accessed 17 March 2012).
20 Carter, *Sir Joseph Banks*, pp. 332–333; Hector Charles Cameron, *Sir Joseph Banks* (Sydney: Angus and Robertson, 1952), p. 125.
21 Natural History Museum, Botany Library, Banksian Collection, MSS BANKS COLL BAN, 'MS. Book of weights of friends and acquaintances', 1788–1814.
22 Agnes Arber, 'Sir Joseph and Botany,' *Annual Biography and Obituary*, 5 (1821), 97–120.
23 Quoted in Chambers, *Joseph Banks and the British Museum*, p. 31.

24 See the chapter by Alice Marples in this volume.
25 Andrew Wilton, 'The Print Room', in *Treasures of the British Museum*, ed. by Frank Francis (London: Thames and Hudson, 1972), p. 293.
26 Henry Ellis, *British Museum Letter Book 1802–1847* (London: British Museum).
27 *Ibid*.
28 See the chapters by Alice Marples and Toby Burrows in this volume.

4 'There never was such a collector since the world began'

A new look at Sir Thomas Phillipps

Toby Burrows

When Sir Thomas Phillipps died in 1872, the *Athenaeum* was fulsome in its obituary for him. Not only was he 'the greatest book collector of modern times'; he was also a 'great scholar' – 'one of the most learned men of the age.' All in all, 'there never was such a collector since the world began.'[1] This obituary was all the more remarkable for having being written by his son-in-law, J. O. Halliwell, from whom he had been bitterly estranged for almost 30 years.[2]

The unparalleled size of his collection is not a matter of hyperbole: it was almost certainly the biggest private manuscript collection ever assembled, and was significantly bigger than most public collections, even today. Estimates of its size vary, from more than 40,000 to 'not far short of sixty thousand' – the latter being the estimate of his grandson, who was in the best position to know. His library also included more than 50,000 printed books and pamphlets.[3]

Phillipps had been born in 1792, the illegitimate son of a Manchester textile manufacturer, and inherited the landed estate at Middle Hill in Gloucestershire acquired by his father. He was raised to a baronetcy in 1821, and spent most of the income from his lands on building his giant collection. The cost was enormous; Phillipps spent something like two-thirds of his income for 50 years on the collection, amounting to somewhere between £200,000 and £250,000 in total, according to an estimate by A. N. L. Munby.[4]

Phillipps was buying manuscripts at a good time. Many private libraries came on the market during the 1820s and 1830s, and many of these had their origins in the libraries of the suppressed Western European religious houses in the later eighteenth and early nineteenth centuries. Not all of these had been legitimately acquired by their previous owners; among the major sources of the Phillipps collection were two Italian collectors whose own acquisitions appear to have involved stealing from municipal

Table 4.1 Major collections absorbed into the Phillipps collection

Collector	*Number of MSS*	*Date*	*Origin*
Van Ess	377	1824	Western, Oriental
Chardin	155	1824	French, German
Celotti	156	1825	Italian, French
Meerman	660	1824	French, German, Dutch
Craven Ord	231	1829–1832	English
Guilford	1,623	1830 ff.	Italian, French
Heber	428	1836	English, French, Flemish
Ranuzzi	71	1847	Italian
Kingsborough	165	1842	Mexican, Spanish
Porter	296	1852	English, South American
Betham	346	1854, 1860	Ulster
Dering	135	1858–1865	English
Libri	217	1849–1865	Italian, French
Newling	164		
Fitch	151	1855–1859	English
Hunter	91	1862	English
Fischer	237	1869–1870	Mexican

and religious libraries in France and Italy: Luigi Celotti and Guglielmo Libri.[5] A summary of the major private collectors whose manuscript collections were the main sources for the Phillipps collection is shown in Table 4.1.

Phillipps seems to have done most of his own collecting and acquisitions. Unlike other major collectors, he did not employ a librarian or a team of specialist agents. His own buying trips to France, Switzerland, Flanders and Germany in 1822–1823 and 1827–1829 were very productive, but were not repeated in later years. Most of his purchases were made in the London auction rooms, either in person or through English book dealers like Thomas Thorpe, Thomas Rodd, Puttick and Simpson and Payne and Foss. His relationships with these men were often fraught, especially because of his continual financial difficulties and lengthy delays in payment. Thorpe, in particular, was almost bankrupted in 1837 by Phillipps's failure to pay promptly.

One important exception was Obadiah Rich, the American consul in Madrid and later Majorca, who was employed by Phillipps in the 1830s as an agent for Spanish materials, though this relationship eventually soured and ended in a legal case. Once Phillipps's reputation began to spread, however, he was frequently approached by people wanting to sell him objects of various kinds. Captain Robert Mignan of the East India Company was one of these; he sold Phillipps a group of Arabic and Persian manuscripts in 1829, together with a cuneiform cylinder of Nebuchadnezzar II – probably the oldest object in the Phillipps collection, which is now on display in the Bodmer Library at Coligny near Geneva. Mignan claimed to have found the cylinder in the Babylonian ruins near the town of Hillah, but is more likely to have removed it from the house in Baghdad of the Catholic-Armenian Vicar-General of Ispahan, given that it was almost certainly the same cylinder transcribed there by Carl Bellino in 1818.[6] Like most of these relationships, the connection with Mignan ended with the threat of legal action when Phillipps refused to buy a second consignment of Babylonian materials from him.[7]

The Phillipps collection was notable for its sheer size, and included a substantial number of documents and papers, which ranged in date from medieval through to the nineteenth century. But he also owned beautiful and valuable manuscript codices, many of which are among the treasures of the modern collections where they now reside. A notable example is the so-called Crusader Bible, which the expert Sydney Cockerell called a 'priceless masterpiece' – 'the most splendidly planned and executed of all the wonderful French manuscripts of the thirteenth century.'[8] This manuscript, with its remarkable images of Old Testament stories in thirteenth-century clothing, has a rich history. Made in the mid-thirteenth century, probably for Louis IX of France (Saint Louis), it was almost certainly in Naples by the beginning of the fourteenth century, when Latin captions were added to each image. It is next recorded in Krakow in 1604, in the possession of Cardinal Bernard Maciejowski, when he handed it over to a group of papal envoys on a mission from Pope Clement VIII to the Shah of Persia, Abbas I the Great. From 1608 it was in the possession of the Shah in Isfahan, where Persian captions and a Hebrew transliteration were subsequently added.

Lost after the sack of Isfahan by the Afghans in 1722, the manuscript turned up again in the early nineteenth century in Egypt, where it was bought for three schillings by a Greek dealer in antiquities known as Giovanni d'Athanasi. He sold it at Sotheby's in 1833 to the booksellers Payne and Foss, for 255 guineas, and they in their turn sold it to Phillipps. It is now in the Morgan Library in New York, having been bought from Thomas FitzRoy Fenwick in 1916 by J. P. Morgan's librarian Belle da Costa Greene for the staggering amount of £10,000.

The Phillipps manuscript collection was extremely broad in scope, both geographically and chronologically. Among the oldest material was Phillipps MS 16402: 19 fragmentary Coptic papyri, bought from the Libri sale at Sotheby's in 1862. They were part of the archive of St. Pesynthios, Bishop of Koptos/Keft (569–632), and were probably found at a monastic site in Western Thebes in Upper Egypt. They included letters and documents (among them a list of clothes and information about the wages paid to two carpenters), as well as literary and liturgical texts. The papyri formerly in the Phillipps collection are closely connected to a larger set of similar materials in the Musée du Louvre.

These 19 fragments were included in the sale of the residue of the collection to the Robinson Brothers in 1946. By the early 1970s, these documents were being offered for sale by the London antiquities dealer (and founder of the Folio Society) Charles Ede. Their subsequent dispersal around the world can only partly be traced. Two are now in the art collection of the Antwerp-based shipping and logistics company Katoen Natie (685/01–02). One is in the Bancroft Library at the University of California, Berkeley (P. Berk. 01). Another is owned by the Classics Museum of the Australian National University in Canberra (75.01), where its connection with Phillipps was undocumented until fairly recently.[9]

The Phillipps collection was remarkable in its geographical coverage. The holdings of Mexican manuscripts, for example, were substantial and significant. At least 165 of them came from the library of Edward King, Viscount Kingsborough (1795–1837), who produced a series of volumes of facsimiles of early Mesoamerican codices, under the title *Antiquities of Mexico*. Phillipps was acquainted with Kingsborough, having provided an introduction for him to Bodley's Librarian, Bulkeley Bandinel, and lamented his unfortunate death from typhus in a Dublin jail, where he had been imprisoned for debt.[10] More than 25 years later, Phillipps also acquired the original artwork for Kingsborough's facsimiles, produced by Agostino Aglio, an Italian landscape painter (Phillipps MSS 22897–22902).

Another 147 Mexican manuscripts were acquired in the late 1860s from a very different source. Agustín Fischer (1825–1887) was a German Lutheran who emigrated to North America.[11] By 1852 he had moved to Mexico and become a Catholic priest. He eventually became an adviser and counsellor to the Emperor Maximilian. After Maximilian's execution in June 1867, Fischer returned to Europe. He had collected a large number of Mexican books, manuscripts and artefacts, many of which were sold in London by the booksellers Puttick and Simpson in 1869 and 1870.[12] Fischer returned to Mexico in 1871 and died there in 1887. While some of Phillipps's more than three hundred Mexican manuscripts are now in libraries in the United States, the present whereabouts of many of them are unknown.

The Phillipps collection was also surprisingly rich in Persian, Turkish and Arabic manuscripts and miniatures.[13] Among these were several albums of seventeenth- and eighteenth-century Mughal paintings, two of which had formerly been owned by Warren Hastings (Governor-General of Bengal, 1774–1784) and another by Sir Elijah Impey (Chief Justice of Bengal 1774 to 1783). Unfortunately, the paintings in these albums were sold individually by Sotheby's at two auctions in 1968 and 1974, and are now scattered around the world. A significant number of Phillipps's Persian manuscripts also came from an East India Company source, Captain Robert Mignan, who sold Phillipps 36 manuscripts in 1829. Other Persian and Indian manuscripts came from English collectors, such as John Haddon Hindley and the 4th Marquess of Hastings. There were also some Turkish manuscripts, from the collection of Auguste Chardin, and Arabic manuscripts from Egypt, Syria and North Africa.

One of the most interesting items was a Persian manuscript recording astronomical observations from the observatory at Maragheh (Iran), dated 1288/1289 (Phillipps MS 16354). Bought at the Libri sale in 1859, it is also notable for having 'the earliest decorated Persian binding on a dated manuscript.'[14] It was sold at Sotheby's in 1968 to the Anglo-Iranian dealer and collector Mehdi Mahboubian. One of Phillipps's Arabic manuscripts has travelled further than almost any of the items in his collection: a Coptic Egyptian copy of the Kitāb al-Tawrāh (Torah), written in 1713. It was acquired by Phillipps in 1868 from the booksellers Puttick and Simpson (Phillipps MS 19375). It is now in the Dunedin Public Library, New Zealand, which bought it in 1982 from the London bookseller Alan G. Thomas.[15]

Such a huge collection proved difficult to manage and document, unsurprisingly. The manuscripts were housed in more than 2,000 specially designed wooden boxes, three of which survive today in the collection of the Grolier Club in New York. The boxes were of a standard length (four feet), but their height and width varied from four inches to two feet. They were intended to enable rapid removal of books and manuscripts in the event of a fire, and were piled up throughout the rooms at Middle Hill 'to a convenient height.' Even after the collection was moved to the larger surroundings of Thirlestaine House in Cheltenham in 1863 – a major event which took eight months and at least 105 wagon-loads – Phillipps's wife complained of being 'booked out' of the house.[16]

The arrangement of the collection was described in a letter from Samuel Gael, one of Phillipps's trustees, to Edward Bond of the British Museum, who carried out a valuation for probate after Phillipps's death.[17] The manuscripts were numbered consecutively in approximate order of acquisition, and marked with Phillipps's ownership stamp, a lion rampant. Each box was also given a number, and a finding-list (the 'MSS Reference Book') was used to match manuscript numbers to box numbers. There was another book listing each box by number and showing which room it was in (the 'Box Reference Book'). To find a manuscript involved the following steps:

- Using the printed catalogue to find the number of the manuscript;
- Looking up this number in the 'MSS Reference Book' to find its box number;

- Looking up the box number in the 'Box Reference Book' to find its room and 'site in the Room.'

No wonder many of the manuscripts got out of sequence or could not be found during the probate process! Gael notes: 'Many of the MSS were not found in their Places in the Catalogue.' There were also 'MSS lying in Heaps on the floors unsorted & uncatalogued,' as well as 'several large Portfolios of Deeds uncatalogued.'

Nevertheless, Phillipps spent much time and energy on preparing and printing a catalogue of his manuscripts, beginning from 1837 and ending in 1871 – the year before his death. The complicated printing history of this *Catalogus Librorum Manuscriptorum in Bibliotheca D. Thomae Phillipps, Bart.* has been explored by A. N. L. Munby, who oversaw an invaluable facsimile edition in 1968.[18] The *Catalogus* is difficult to use; the descriptions are often short and unreliable, a single number may cover a whole group of volumes or documents, and some numbers were reassigned and manuscripts renumbered. Phillipps provided indexes to several sections of the catalogue, and also supplied indications of provenance, but these too can be unreliable and hard to navigate.

The *Catalogus* ceases with manuscript number 23,837. Documentation for higher numbers is almost non-existent, though three copies of handwritten inventories made for probate after Phillipps's death have survived. Two of these go up to 26,179 and the third to 26,365. The latter copy was used by Thomas FitzRoy Fenwick to record which manuscripts had been sold, and it was extensively revised and amended by him over the course of five decades. It is not entirely clear which numbers were assigned by Phillipps himself, and which were assigned after his death. But a note inside the cover of the shorter probate inventory suggests that all numbers higher than 23,837 were assigned after Phillipps's death: 'Catalogue of MSS. in Thirlstaine [sic] Library that had never been catalogued by Sir Thos. Phillipps or had lost their Catalogue numbers.'[19] Some of these were assigned during the probate process, and others subsequently to that.

The collection was clearly meant to be used, and Phillipps was surprisingly hospitable to scholars, despite his prickly reputation. Various visitors left enthusiastic accounts of their visits to Middle Hill and of the welcome they received, although several did comment on the somewhat chaotic arrangements there. The American historian Jared Sparks, who visited Middle Hill in 1840, was very complimentary:[20]

> I have rarely passed so agreeable and profitable a week. Sir Thomas Phillipps is renowned for his hospitality, and on this occasion it was bestowed in the most liberal and generous manner.

Even scholars like the future Cardinal Pitra (in 1849) were welcomed, despite Phillipps's very vocal hostility to the Catholic Church. In all, Phillipps corresponded quite extensively with more than 50 scholars in the 1840s and 1850s.

Phillipps made his own contributions to scholarship – although these were mostly those of the amateur wealthy antiquarian, fairly typical of the earlier nineteenth century. He published at least 557 different items between 1818/1819 and 1871, including more than 300 editions and transcriptions of documents relating to local history, genealogy and folklore, and indexes to historical sources.[21] In many cases, his three daughters provided the basic labour of transcription. He ran his own printing press and employed his own printers, though the relationship was often a difficult one.

Phillipps was also actively involved in the world of learned societies. He was elected a Fellow of the Royal Society in 1820 and served as a proposer for William Henry Fox Talbot in 1831 and Frederic Madden in 1832. He was also a Fellow of the Society of Antiquaries and of the Royal Society for Literature and was appointed as a Trustee of the British Museum in 1861. He was particularly interested in the work of the Record Commission and the management of the public records and gave lengthy evidence to the 1836 Buller committee of inquiry into these subjects.

Phillipps came up with a number of different proposals for the disposal of his collection, which he clearly saw as valuable for posterity and the nation.[22] As early as 1827–1828, he approached the University of Oxford to buy his library for £30,000 – though the University rejected his conditions, which included allowing him to manage the library and remove any of the books or manuscripts. He then offered the collection to the British Museum in 1828, and again in 1831; the asking price on the latter occasion was £60,000. By 1850 he was being courted by the Royal Institution in Swansea, but this came to nothing. Negotiations with Oxford began again in 1852 and continued until 1861. This time Phillipps asked for the Ashmolean building, and then the Radcliffe Camera, and eventually proposed that he be appointed Bodley's Librarian. His last unsuccessful move was an attempt to persuade Benjamin Disraeli, then Chancellor of the Exchequer, to sponsor an Act of Parliament which would have established his library as a permanent public institution.

In the end, his complicated will left the collection in trust to his youngest daughter Katharine Fenwick and her husband, to be retained and made available for access at Thirlestaine House. This arrangement quickly proved to be financially and logistically unviable, and the Fenwicks successfully applied to the courts under the new Settled Land Act of 1882 for permission to dispose of the collection. This law enabled heirlooms settled in trust to be sold by the heirs:

> Where personal chattels are settled on trust so as to devolve with land until a tenant in tail by purchase is born or attains the age of twenty-one years, or so as otherwise to vest in some person becoming entitled to an estate of freehold of inheritance in the land, a tenant for life of the land may sell the chattels or any of them.[23]

Most of the subsequent disposal of the manuscripts was managed by their son, Thomas FitzRoy Fenwick. He was very shrewd and careful in selling off manuscripts gradually, through a long series of auctions at Sotheby's, accompanied by occasional direct sales to specific countries or collectors. There were 16 Sotheby's sales between 1886 and 1913, with a total of 18,876 lots realizing £71,277. Six further sales between 1919 and 1938 realized £25,786 from a total of 3,321 lots.[24]

After Fenwick's death in 1938, the remainder of the collection was stored in the basement of Thirlestaine House for the duration of the War, following which his family sold it to the London book dealers Lionel and Philip Robinson. The Robinson brothers offered some of the manuscripts in sales catalogues published between 1948 and 1954, together with consigning others for sale by Sotheby's and Hodgson's at 12 auctions between 1946 and 1958.[25] By 1957, the remaining manuscripts, documents and books were owned by the Robinson Trust, which the Robinson brothers formed after winding up their book-selling business in December 1956. A new series of 20 Sotheby's auctions was held on behalf of the Trust between 1966 and 1981. The remaining material, estimated to contain at least 2,000 manuscripts and over 130,000 letters and documents, was sold to the American dealer H. P. Kraus in 1977.[26] Kraus advertised the first installment of a 'final selection' from the Phillipps collection in a catalogue of 1979.[27]

Phillipps manuscripts are still being advertised for sale today on sites like AbeBooks as well as through auctions held by large and small dealers alike. A significant proportion of the collection is in private hands, and much of it is now difficult or impossible to trace. But it is clear that the Phillipps manuscripts have been dispersed all over the world – enriching collections in North America, Japan, Australia and New Zealand as well as across Western Europe. Cultural institutions of all types have benefited: libraries, museums, galleries, archives and local record offices.

Tracing this dispersal is a Herculean task. Several methods for collating the relevant information have been tried, notably by A. N. L. Munby, the author of the definitive study of Phillipps as a collector. In 1955, working in collaboration with L. J. Gorton, Munby began a card index which is now held in the Manuscripts Reading Room of the British Library.[28] By the time of Munby's preface to the 1968 facsimile edition of the *Catalogus Librorum Manuscriptorum*, this card index contained more than 10,000 locations. It was still being updated by British Library staff in the 1990s, but has never been digitized and is not always reliable or accurate.

Munby also used interleaved pages in a copy of the *Catalogus Librorum Manuscriptorum* to note references to sales and auction catalogues and to library holdings of individual manuscripts. His original annotated catalogue, bound in three volumes, is now in a private collection in the United States. A microfilm copy was made in 1975 for the Cambridge University Library; the Bodleian Library has a photocopy made from this microfilm. The Bodleian copy continued to be updated by Library staff until at least the 1990s. None of these copies has been digitized, and all of them now differ from the British Library's card index in the information they provide. The Institut de recherche et d'histoire des textes (IRHT) in Paris has its own typescript index of Phillipps locations, compiled by Edith Brayer in 1951.[29]

Phillipps was not just a collector of manuscripts, however and not everything listed in his printed catalogue and given a number was a manuscript or a document. He owned somewhere between 1,600 and 1,800 Old Master drawings, for a start. Many of them had originally been part of the vast collection assembled by the painter Sir Thomas Lawrence, which was later owned by the Woodburn brothers. Phillipps bought over 1,000 of these drawings at Christie's in 1860.

In the mid-1930s, A. E. Popham compiled a catalogue of about 1,250 drawings still owned by the Fenwick family.[30] These drawings were clearly of very mixed quality and value, and Popham left uncatalogued about 400 of them, which he described as those too badly damaged to be recognizable, obviously inferior copies of famous artists, and 'a vast number of unnamed and unnameable scraps.' But the drawings have found their way into various major institutional collections, both in Britain and in the United States, after they were sold off in the 1930s and 1940s. Many ended up in the British Museum, and others are in the Courtauld Gallery. The latter group were purchased from the Fenwick family after the war by Count Antoine Seilern, and bequeathed to the Courtauld after his death in 1978. Seilern was definitely a connoisseur of Old Master drawings, and his collection was one of the best of the post-war era. Some of the Old Master drawings, including those now owned by the Metropolitan Museum of Art in New York, were listed and numbered in Phillipps's manuscript catalogue, suggesting that he had a broad approach to defining a 'manuscript'; drawings were, after all, drawn by hand.

Phillipps also collected oil paintings and water-colours. The most detailed list, compiled in 1869, contains 370 works in all.[31] One of the advantages of his move to Thirlestaine House was that he gained enough space to display his art collection. Middle Hill was too small, as the surviving lists of paintings make clear, and a number of them had to be stored in the house-keeper's room. In fact, Phillipps bought about 100 paintings from the estate of the previous owner of Thirlestaine, Lord Northwick, in 1860 – a purchase which Frederic Madden described in his journal as 'the act of an idiot.'[32] One explanation is that Phillipps was following the same approach as he had with manuscripts: trying to keep together earlier collections in the face of their dispersal.

One of the rooms at Thirlestaine House was devoted to the paintings of George Catlin (1796–1872). Catlin was an American artist turned entrepreneur; he specialized in paintings of Native Americans, and spent many years in Britain and France touring his 'Indian Gallery' – which consisted not only of paintings but also of several Native Americans in person.[33] Phillipps was Catlin's patron during the 1840s and 1850s, and actually lent him money more than once – a very untypical act for Phillipps. There was a long-standing correspondence between them, which survives on opposite sides of the Atlantic – in the Bodleian Library and in Tulsa, Oklahoma, at the Gilcrease Museum of Western Art.

Phillipps had two sets of Catlin's paintings, both of which are now in the Gilcrease Museum and both of which were acquired in repayment of Phillipps's loans to Catlin. The first consisted of watercolour portraits of Native Americans, 70 in total, which were given individual Phillipps numbers in the *Catalogus*. The other set of paintings consisted of copies made by Catlin for Phillipps of many of the paintings in his Indian Gallery, showing Indian ceremonies and landscapes of the Mid-West. There are 57 of these oil paintings, which also have individual Phillipps numbers in the printed catalogue.

Catlin was a significant early artist of the American West, whose Indian Gallery is now in the Smithsonian Museum. His relationship with Phillipps reveals an unexpected side to Phillipps as a collector. His tastes and interests evidently ran well beyond the antiquarian and the purely European. Perhaps the opportunity to exercise patronage was also a significant motivation? This is reinforced by another of the rooms at Thirlestaine House, known as the Glover Gallery and dedicated to the works of the landscape painter John Glover (1767–1849). Phillipps was also something of a patron to Glover and owned nearly 50 of his paintings. Their earliest connection seems to date from 1824, when Phillipps commissioned Glover to paint three views of Middle Hill. There is a series of letters between the two men in the Phillipps papers in the Bodleian Library, and Phillipps later reprinted copies of several of Glover's exhibition catalogues.

Glover is a relatively minor figure in the history of English landscape painting in the earlier nineteenth century. But he is much more significant – and much better known – in Australia. He migrated to Van Diemen's Land (Tasmania) in 1831 at the age of 64, and his subsequent Australian paintings were the first serious attempts to paint the Australian landscape in a European style. The Art Gallery of New South Wales describes him as 'one of Australia's most celebrated colonial landscape painters'; he is 'significant for being the first painter of the Australian landscape sensitive to its visual and spatial qualities and its latent expressive potential.'[34]

When Glover sent a consignment of his first Tasmanian paintings back to London for an exhibition in 1835, Phillipps bought at least three of them.[35] One, showing Glover's garden in northern Tasmania near Launceston, was acquired in 1951 by the Art Gallery of South Australia in Adelaide.[36] Another Glover painting, which is also in the Art Gallery of South Australia, is very significant as the first European painting of an Aboriginal corroboree, painted in 1832 – although all the remaining Aboriginal Tasmanians had been moved to Flinders Island by 1833, so it is unclear whether Glover was painting from direct observation. In the handwritten catalogue of pictures at Thirlestaine House in 1869, it is described as being located at the Swan River, though there is no record of Glover ever travelling to the Western side of Australia.

As well as listing some of his paintings and drawings among his manuscripts, Phillipps included several photograph albums in the *Catalogus*. He describes these as 'manuscripts by the hand of nature,' an interesting expression of what quickly became the standard contemporary view of the role of photography.[37] The surviving albums are now in the Houghton Library at Harvard University. Most of them are photographs commissioned by Phillipps, rather than photographic prints acquired by him, and consist of views of trees and other objects on the Middle Hill estate.

Two of the albums are particularly interesting since they contain photographs of manuscripts and objects in the Phillipps Collection, taken in the early 1850s by Mrs Amelia Guppy. She seems to have been an amateur photographer, and the surviving negatives and prints are full of trials and errors. But these are some of the earliest attempts to use photographs to document museum objects and manuscripts. One of the manuscripts she photographed was the thirteenth-century Welsh Book of Aneirin, one of the Four Ancient Books of Wales (Phillipps MS 16614) – now Cardiff MS 2.81, on deposit in the National Library of Wales since 2011 and available online in full digital colour since 2013.

Photography was not the only innovative technique used by Phillipps in documenting his collections. He was also an early adopter of anastatic printing, which was developed in the 1840s as a form of transfer lithography. It could be used to reproduce drawings and handwriting easily and quickly, avoiding the need for expensive and time-consuming engraving and typesetting. Phillipps made considerable use of it in his Middle Hill publications, particularly for publishing his transcriptions of parish registers and other types of historical documents.[38] He also unsuccessfully urged the Rolls Office and the Record Office to use it for transcribing government records.[39] No doubt the much lower cost appealed to him, as much as the way in which delays and difficulties in printing could be reduced.

Phillipps was relatively reticent about the aims and motives which inspired him to amass such a huge collection. His only written statement was in the unpublished draft of a preface to his printed catalogue (written c. 1828), which is worth quoting at length:[40]

> In amassing my Collection of MSS. I commenced with purchasing everything that lay within my reach, to which I was instigated by reading various accounts of the destruction of valuable MSS. As in the beginning of any undertaking few persons are sufficiently masters of their subject as to judge unerringly what may be done & what not done so with regard to myself; I had not the ability to select, nor the resolution to let anything escape because it was of trifling value. My principal search has been for Historical & particularly unpublished MSS., whether good or bad, and more particularly those on vellum. My chief desire for preserving Vellum MSS. arose from witnessing the unceasing destruction of them by Goldbeaters; My search for charters or deeds by their destruction in the shops of Glue-makers & Taylors.
>
> As I advanced, the ardour of pursuit increased untill at last I became a perfect Vello-maniac (if I may coin a word) and I gave any price that was asked. Nor do I regret it, for my object was not only to secure good Manuscripts for myself but also to raise the public estimation of them, so that their value might be more generally known, & consequently more MSS. preserved. For nothing tends to the preservation of anything so much as making it bear a high price.
>
> The examples I always kept in view were Sir Robert Cotton & Sir. Robt. Harley. They had the advantage of me in living a century or two before, & although their collections were so immense, that some thought there was nothing to be gleaned after them, yet I foresaw that there must be vast treasures upon the Continent in consequence of the dispersion of Monastic libraries by the French Revolution. In this I was not deceived.... And although I have amassed above three thousand volumes in the course of six years, yet any other person equally devoted, & with the same fortune would collect as many more in the same space of time. I do not intend to cease collecting, although I shall for the future diminish my ardour, because I have raised MSS. to their proper value.

He goes on to claim that the bookseller Thomas Thorpe (one of his main suppliers) hardly ever dealt in manuscripts until Phillipps paid him high prices and urged him 'to buy up all he could.' He also discusses the 'melancholy fate' of Sir Robert Cotton's library – the carelessness, apathy and ignorance of the barbarians who destroyed it, and the 'ungrateful return made by the Government to Sir Robert.'

In the unpublished Preface, Phillipps invokes Cotton (1571–1631) and Robert Harley (1661–1724) as his models. There is some obvious truth in this; both Cotton and Harley collected significant numbers of medieval manuscripts and documents. Their interest was clearly historical and antiquarian, rather than the connoisseurship of beautiful objects. Cotton owned more than 950 manuscripts, as well as many rolls, charters and books.[41] Harley seems to have owned about 6,000 volumes, 14,000 medieval and later charters and 500 rolls.[42] To judge from this comparison, Phillipps may have seen himself as something of a latter-day antiquarian, collecting and preserving historical materials for the British nation. Both Cotton's and Harley's manuscript collections had been incorporated into the British Museum, an institution to which Phillipps also had a strong connection and to which he tried to transfer his own collection.

A more interesting comparison, however, is with Harley's son Edward (1689–1741). He extended the family collection dramatically in both size and scope, adding large numbers of pamphlets, prints, pictures, antiquities, bronzes, coins, medals and medallions. C. H. Wright observes that Edward Harley exhibits the way in which tastes were changing in the early eighteenth century: a new interest in material from the Continent, including Greek and Oriental manuscripts.[43] Like Phillipps, Harley spent beyond his means, and was criticized by contemporaries for his indiscriminate approach to collecting. 'There is . . . much rubbish,' Horace Walpole noted acidly in relation to the Harley sales of 1742.[44]

In many ways, though, the most appropriate comparison is with that prodigious collector of the eighteenth century, Sir Hans Sloane. Though his vast collections were primarily of materials relevant to natural history, they included a significant number of manuscripts.[45] Sloane's motives for collecting remained largely unarticulated, but his primary goal seems to have been to accumulate as many unique and rare materials as possible, with their preservation and documentation as priorities. Like Phillipps, he incorporated wholesale the collections of various other people into his own. He was widely criticized for his indiscriminate collecting, and his motives were questioned; he was accused of using his collections for financial gain and social acceptance. He was regarded, not as a connoisseur, but as more of an antiquarian – at a time when connoisseurship was fashionable. He opened up his collections to scholars, but they remained little used. Having only daughters, like Phillipps, he was collecting for posterity and wanted to leave his collections to the nation. Unlike Phillipps, he did manage to ensure that they were acquired as one of the foundational collections of the new British Museum.

In the scale and scope of his manuscript collecting, however, Phillipps went a long way beyond his predecessors. His description of himself as a 'Vello-maniac' in the unpublished Preface is an interesting one, and probably should be read as an ironic nod to Thomas Frognall Dibdin's *Bibliomania, or Book Madness*, first published in 1809.[46] Werner Muensterberger, in his book on collecting, takes it more literally – as a manifestation of Phillipps's 'severe inner problems,' which led him into an obsession with objects which served as 'magical remedies against existential doubt' and as a compensation for the insecurities resulting from his illegitimate birth and lack of maternal care.[47] But the scale and breadth of Phillipps's collecting cannot simply be explained away solely in psychoanalytic terms as a response to his personal circumstances and as a manifestation of his undoubtedly difficult personality. There were more factors at work than that.

Muensterberger's account of Phillipps relies heavily on the work of A. N. L. Munby. In this context, it is perhaps unfortunate that Munby quotes liberally from the journal of Phillipps's contemporary Sir Frederic Madden (1801–1873), Keeper of Manuscripts at the British Museum. In private, Madden took a dim view of Phillipps, describing him (amongst other things) as 'a selfish madman' and 'an arrant fool.'[48] But perhaps these comments say more about Madden; after all, he was privately vitriolic about a whole range of other people, not just Phillipps. His feuds with his colleagues at the British Museum – and especially with its director Antonio Panizzi – were numerous, long-standing and 'Homeric' in scope (in Munby's view).[49] Madden was 'a curmudgeon's curmudgeon if ever there was one, with seldom a good word for anyone,' according to Richard Beadle.[50] In reality, his connection with Phillipps was long-standing and relatively amicable, at least until the 1860s. Phillipps was godson to Madden's son George Phillipps Madden, and later offered a job to Madden's other son Frederic, as well as proposing Madden for the Fellowship of the Royal Society.

A more balanced appraisal must begin from the way in which Phillipps talks about his desire to preserve and rescue as many manuscripts as possible for posterity. There is no reason to doubt his sincerity in saying this. Wishing to be valued for his contribution as an antiquarian on a large scale was clearly one of Phillipps's motives, also demonstrated by his commitment to publishing scholarly materials and by his membership of antiquarian associations. In the unpublished Preface, he also mentions his willingness to drive up prices to achieve his goals, but this had its limits. While he was willing to outbid other buyers – especially the British Museum – in the auction rooms, there were times when he simply refused to pay what he felt were unreasonably high prices.

Although Madden and others disparaged him as no connoisseur, and a collector of 'rubbish and fragments,' his collection was not simply about quantity. He owned his fair share of beautiful and valuable manuscripts, which are now among the treasures of institutions like the Morgan Library and many of which were eagerly sought by subsequent generations of connoisseur collectors from Sydney Cockerell to Alfred Chester Beatty.[51] Others of his manuscripts are of great value for their significance as witnesses to the history of countries across Western Europe, as well as in North and Central America. A. N. L. Munby tried to select his 'top thirty' manuscripts from the Phillipps collection, but admitted this was an almost impossible task.[52]

While Phillipps did not come from a long line of landed or titled gentry, he lived like a gentleman, relying on his income from his estates and focusing his life on historical, antiquarian and literary activities. Although his father had made his fortune in trade, Phillipps was hardly one of the 'nouveaux riches' described so vividly by J. Mordaunt Crook.[53] He certainly shared many of the opinions of conservative landowners, especially in his strident anti-Catholicism, and his opposition to Free Trade and the repeal of the Corn Laws. He may well have considered that collecting would help to demonstrate that he was a gentleman, and allay any doubts about his somewhat unorthodox origins. In a superficial sense he was part of the established tradition of the country house library and the connoisseurship of the landed gentry.[54] But the scale of his collecting, and the purpose he claimed for it, went well beyond this tradition. They place him within a different world, that of the wealthy antiquarian and amateur, at a time when that world was changing with the emergence of professional and institutional experts like Sir Frederic Madden and Henry Bradshaw.[55]

When we add in Phillipps's other activities – especially his patronage of artists like Catlin and Glover, and his interest in early photography and anastatic printing, especially for copying and documenting manuscripts and objects – the result is a collector who, in some ways, harks back to the vast scope and ambition of eighteenth-century collectors like Sloane, but in other ways is very much a man of his time. The combination of these two perspectives helps to explain the scale and importance of his collecting. But perhaps, like Christopher Wren, his achievement is best assessed by looking around at the public manuscript collections of the world. His manuscripts form significant and valuable components of many major national and university libraries, as well as in regional record offices and in the specialist libraries founded by the great manuscript collectors of the twentieth century like Morgan, Huntington and Folger. Without the dispersal of his vast collection, the manuscript market of the last 130 years would have been much smaller and less active. Because his library was scattered across the globe, and he left no institutional legacy of his own, he is largely unknown to the general public. But he was undoubtedly the most important and extraordinary manuscript collector of the nineteenth century.

Notes

1 'Art and Literary Gossip: Sir Thomas Phillipps, Bart,' *Manchester Weekly Times – Supplement* (17 February 1872), p. 56.
2 A. N. L. Munby, *The Family Affairs of Sir Thomas Phillipps* (Phillipps Studies, No. 2) (Cambridge: Cambridge University Press, 1952), p. 100.
3 A. N. L. Munby, *The Formation of the Phillipps Library from 1841 to 1872* (Phillipps Studies, No. 4) (Cambridge, UK: Cambridge University Press, 1956), p. 166.
4 *Ibid.*, p. 167.
5 Anne-Marie Eze, *Abbé Luigi Celotti (1759–1843): Connoisseur, Dealer, and Collector of Illuminated Miniatures* (London: Courtauld Institute of Art, 2010) [doctoral thesis]; P. Alessandra Maccioni Ruju and Marco Mostert, *The Life and Times of Guglielmo Libri (1802–1869), Scientist, Patriot, Scholar, Journalist and Thief: A Nineteenth-Century Story* (Hilversum: Verloren, 1995).
6 Robert Mignan, *Travels in Chaldaea* (London: Colburn and Bentley, 1829), pp. 228–229; William Henry Fox Talbot, 'Translation of an Inscription of Nebuchadnezzar,' *Transactions of the Royal Society of Literature*, Series 2, 7 (1862), 341–375.
7 A. N. L. Munby, *The Formation of the Phillipps Library Up to the Year 1840* (Phillipps Studies, No. 3) (Cambridge, UK: Cambridge University Press, 1954), p. 56.
8 Sydney C. Cockerell, 'The Book and Its History,' in *A Book of Old Testament Illustrations of the Middle of the Thirteenth Century* (Cambridge, UK: Cambridge University Press for the Roxburghe Club, 1972), pp. 57, 72 – see also Stella Panayotova's chapter in this volume.
9 Benjamin Kelly, 'A Late-Antique Contract in the Collection of the Australian National University Classics Museum,' *Zeitschrift für Papyrologie und Epigraphik*, 161 (2007), 207–214.
10 A. N. L. Munby, *The Formation of the Phillipps Library from 1841 to 1872*, p. 12.
11 Álvaro Canales Santos, *Agustín Fischer, el rasputín de II Imperio Mexicano* (Saltillo, Coah.: Club del Libro Coahuilense, El Dos, 2005).
12 A. N. L. Munby, *The Formation of the Phillipps Library from 1841 to 1872*, p. 138.
13 J. Michael Rogers, 'Great Britain xi: Persian Art Collections in Britain,' *Encyclopaedia Iranica*, www.iranicaonline.org/articles/great-britain-xi (accessed 23 February 2012).
14 Sotheby & Co., *Catalogue of Persian, Turkish and Arabic Manuscripts, Indian and Persian Miniatures* (Bibliotheca Phillippica, New Series: Medieval Manuscripts, 4th Part) (London: Sotheby & Co., 1968), p. 63.
15 Dunedin Public Libraries, Reed MS 11.
16 A. N. L. Munby, *The Family Affairs of Sir Thomas Phillipps*, p. 91.

17 Samuel Gael, Letter to Edward Bond, 17 April 1872 (Grolier Club, *Phillipps Collection*).
18 Sir Thomas Phillipps, *The Phillipps Manuscripts: Catalogus Librorum Manuscriptorum in Bibliotheca D. Thomae Phillipps, Bart* (London: Holland Press, 1968).
19 Grolier Club, *Phillipps Collection*, MS Cat. 14.
20 A. N. L. Munby, *The Formation of the Phillipps Library from 1841 to 1872*, p. 32.
21 Martin Antonetti and Eric Holzenberg, 'The Horblit Phillipps Collection at the Grolier Club,' *The Gazette of the Grolier Club*, 48 (1997), 51–72.
22 A. N. L. Munby, *The Dispersal of the Phillipps Library* (Phillipps Studies, No. 5) (Cambridge, UK: Cambridge University Press, 1960), pp. 2–12.
23 *Settled Land Act 1872*, 45 & 46 Vict. Ch. 38, section 37 (1), www.legislation.gov.uk/ukpga/1882/38/pdfs/ukpga_18820038_en.pdf
24 Five of these sales were of printed books, the rest of manuscripts and autograph letters. A. N. L. Munby, *The Dispersal of the Phillipps Library*, pp. 55, 86.
25 A. N. L. Munby, *The Dispersal of the Phillipps Library*, pp. 106–107.
26 Hans P. Kraus, *A Rare Book Saga: The Autobiography of H.P. Kraus* (New York: Putnam, 1978), p. 226.
27 Hans P. Kraus, *Bibliotheca Phillippica: Manuscripts on Vellum and Paper from the 9th to the 18th Centuries, from the Celebrated Collection Formed by Sir Thomas Phillipps: The Final Selection* (Catalogue No 153) (New York: H. P. Kraus, 1979).
28 A. N. L. Munby, *The Formation of the Phillipps Library from 1841 to 1872*, p. xii.
29 Edith Brayer, *Dispersion des manuscrits de la Collection Phillipps jadis conservée à Cheltenham: tables de concordance* (Paris: IRHT, 1951).
30 Thomas FitzRoy Phillipps Fenwick and Arthur Ewart Popham, *Catalogue of Drawings in the Collection Formed by Sir Thomas Phillipps, Bart., F.R.S., Now in the Possession of His Grandson, T. Fitzroy Phillipps Fenwick of Thirlestaine House, Cheltenham* (London: Priv. print. for T. FitzRoy Fenwick, 1935).
31 *Catalogue of Phillipps Gallery 1869* (Bodleian Library, MS Phillipps-Robinson c.696).
32 A. N. L. Munby, *The Formation of the Phillipps Library*, p. 225.
33 Joan Carpenter Troccoli, 'George Catlin and Sir Thomas Phillipps: A Nineteenth-Century Friendship,' *Rare Books and Manuscripts Librarianship*, 10 (1995), 9–20.
34 Art Gallery of New South Wales, 'John Glover: Artist Profile', www.artgallery.nsw.gov.au/collection/artists/glover-john/
35 *A Catalogue of Pictures Descriptive of Van Diemen's Land . . . by John Glover* (1835) (Bodleian Library, MS Phillipps-Robinson d.323).
36 David Hansen, *John Glover and the Colonial Picturesque* (Hobart: Tasmanian Museum and Art Gallery, 2003).
37 Larry J. Schaaf, '"Splendid Calotypes": Henry Talbot, Amelia Guppy, Sir Thomas Phillipps, and Photographs on Paper,' in *Six Exposures: Essays in Celebration of the Opening of the Harrison D. Horblit Collection of Early Photography* (Cambridge, MA: Houghton Library, Harvard University, 1999), pp. 21–46.
38 Geoffrey Wakeman, 'Anastatic Printing for Sir Thomas Phillipps,' *Journal of the Printing Historical Society*, 5 (1969), 24–40.
39 A. N. L. Munby, *The Formation of the Phillipps Library*, p. 110.

40 Printed from the manuscript in the Grolier Club, New York, by A. N. L. Munby, *The Catalogues of Manuscripts and Printed Books of Sir Thomas Phillipps* (Phillipps Studies, No. 1) (Cambridge: Cambridge University Press, 1951), pp. 18–20.
41 Kevin Sharpe, *Sir Robert Cotton, 1586–1631: History and Politics in Early Modern England* (Oxford: Oxford University Press, 1979), p. 75.
42 Derek Adlam, *The Great Collector: Edward Harley, 2nd Earl of Oxford* (Welbeck: The Harley Gallery, 2013), p. 8.
43 Cyril Ernest Wright, *Fontes Harleiani* (London: British Museum, 1972).
44 Adlam, *The Great Collector*, p. 45.
45 James Delbourgo, *Collecting the World: The Life and Curiosity of Hans Sloane* (London: Allen Lane, 2017); see also the essay by Alice Marples in this volume.
46 Thomas Frognall Dibdin, *Bibliomania, or Book Madness: A Bibliographical Romance* (London: Printed for the Author, 1809).
47 Werner Muensterberger, *Collecting: An Unruly Passion: Psychological Perspectives* (Princeton, NJ: Princeton University Press, 1994), pp. 73–100.
48 A. N. L. Munby, *The Formation of the Phillipps Library from 1841 to 1872*, p. 102.
49 A. N. L. Munby, 'Three Opportunities,' in *Essays and Papers*, ed. by Nicholas Barker (London: The Scolar Press, 1977), pp. 141–150 (originally published in *The Book Collector*, 15.4 (Winter 1966)).
50 Richard Beadle, *Henry Bradshaw and the Foundations of Codicology: The Sandars Lectures 2015* (Cambridge: Richard Beadle, 2017), p. 71, note 7.
51 On these, see the chapters by Laura Cleaver and Danielle Magnusson and Stella Panayotova in this volume.
52 A. N. L. Munby, *The Formation of the Phillipps Library*, pp. 161–164.
53 J. Mordaunt Crook, *The Rise of the Nouveaux Riches* (London: John Murray, 2000).
54 Mark Purcell, *The Country House Library* (New Haven: Yale University Press, 2017); Mark Girouard, *The Victorian Country House* (New Haven, CT and London: Yale University Press, 1979).
55 Alan Bell, 'The Journal of Sir Frederic Madden, 1852,' *The Library*, Series 5, 29 (1974), 405–421; Beadle, *Henry Bradshaw and the Foundations of Codicology*.

5 American collectors and the trade in medieval illuminated manuscripts in London, 1919–1939

J. P. Morgan Junior, A. Chester Beatty and Bernard Quaritch Ltd.

Laura Cleaver and Danielle Magnusson

> You ask me if there are any collectors in England except Dyson Perrins. Well really he is the only man who would spend £15000 or £20000 at a sale, but on the other hand there are at least half a dozen people who would be quite willing to buy one fine manuscript at a cost of say two or three thousand pounds just for the sake of possessing one really good specimen of early art.
>
> (E. H. Dring, letter to Belle da Costa Greene, 8 May 1919)[1]

The trade in illuminated medieval manuscripts in Britain and America between the two world wars was dominated by a very small group of collectors. These men and women relied heavily on the advice and services of those working in museums and as dealers. The Morgan Library in New York preserves a large collection of correspondence between its librarian (and later director) Belle da Costa Greene and the directors of the London-based book dealer Bernard Quaritch Ltd: Edmund H. Dring (d. 1928) and his successor Frederic Sutherland Ferguson.[2] In addition to instructions for the purchase of books, the letters contain comments on rival collectors and dealers, together with other news and gossip.[3] In 1919, in the wake of the First World War, and in advance of the sale of the first portion of the famous collection of medieval manuscripts created by Henry Yates Thompson, Greene sought Dring's opinion on the state of the market for manuscripts. On 22 June 1919, she wrote again to Dring, declaring:

> I think Mr. Chester Beatty has a very fine appreciation of manuscripts and will end up being a serious rival to us, some day. There is no-one over

> here who either knows or *even suspects* anything about fine M.S.S. and, for that reason it is a great pleasure to meet a real connoisseur.[4]

Beatty and his wife Edith were visiting America at the time, where they had presumably met Greene and visited the Morgan Library. Dring responded: 'I am glad you like Mr. Chester Beatty. He really has a very good knowledge of manuscripts,' and in a talk given in 1978, Dring's son identified Morgan and Beatty as amongst Quaritch's most important clients in the interwar period.[5] Alfred Chester Beatty was American by birth, but having made his fortune as a mining engineer and following the death of his first wife in 1911, he moved to London, where he married his compatriot Edith Dunn in 1913.[6] In the same year J. P. Morgan Senior died, leaving his extensive collection of artworks to his son, J. P. Morgan Junior, known as Jack. Greene continued in her role as librarian, becoming director of the Morgan Library in 1924, when it became a public institution.

There was considerable concern in Britain in the early twentieth century about the export of artworks, and American collectors were often characterized as rich, but undiscerning. Morgan Senior was depicted in one cartoon with a giant magnet in the form of a dollar sign, attracting a wide range of objects, including books (see Figure 5.1). After the sale of the first portion of the Yates Thompson collection in 1919, Sydney Cockerell, director of the Fitzwilliam Museum in Cambridge, and a collector of

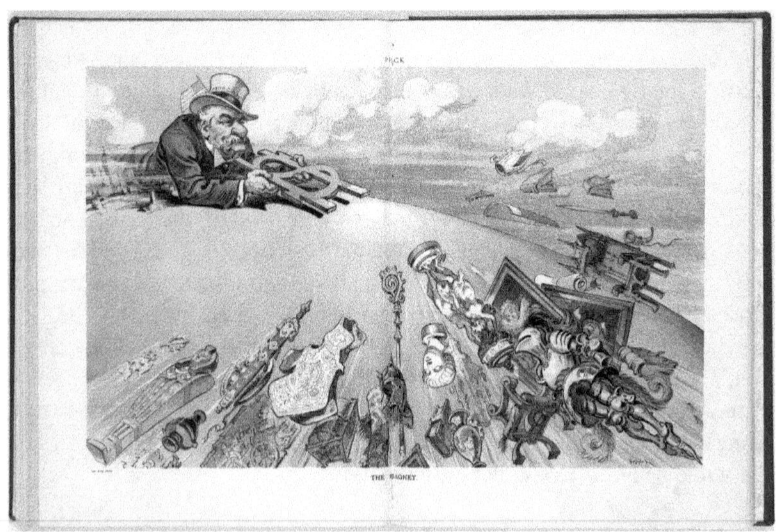

Figure 5.1 J. Keppler Jr., 'The Magnet,' *Puck Magazine*, 1911
Library of Congress, www.loc.gov/item/98518211

manuscripts in his own right, recorded in his diary that he 'went to Quaritch's to gossip with Dring about yesterday's sale. Was relieved to find that many of the MSS will stay in England.'[7] At the same time, dealers, including the staff at Quaritch, actively sought to interest collectors like Morgan in manuscripts, and a week after his conversation with Cockerell, Dring wrote to Greene offering her volumes from the Yates Thompson sale.[8] Concentrating on Morgan Jr. and Beatty as two very different, though contemporary, American collectors of illuminated manuscripts, this chapter will explore the ways in which their collecting practices were shaped by their relationships with those in the book trade, and in particular with Bernard Quaritch Ltd.

American collectors

In a 1927 article entitled 'Why America Buys England's Books,' Dr. A. S. W. Rosenbach, the preeminent American dealer in illuminated manuscripts of the era, referred to the movement of manuscripts and rare books from England to America as a 'magic exodus.'[9] Rosenbach was responding to very real anxieties concerning the numbers of English cultural treasures being absorbed by rapidly growing American libraries. The *Times* of London lamented in 1906 that, 'thanks to the unlimited commissions of two or three rival American collectors, it seems hopeless for English collectors to attempt to enter the arena in the face of such odds.'[10] In the same year *The New York Times* declared that 'the thought of treasure after treasure being carried away to the land of the uncouth is dispiriting to the cultured Briton.'[11] While Rosenbach insisted that the British Museum had managed to remain 'the largest and most important library in the world,' he also described the situation as inexorable, since 'rare books and the precious things of the collector follow the flow of gold.'[12] He went on to reassure readers that 'the traditional Englishman has been so accustomed to seeing about him the finest things of art and literature that in the course of years he becomes a trifle bored.'[13] Should these items be missed at any point, they could simply be reclaimed by Englishmen 'in shops in Philadelphia, in New Orleans, in Minneapolis, in San Francisco.'[14] Unlike other European countries, Britain did not introduce laws to restrict the export of manuscripts until 1939.[15]

American collectors, however, were often hesitant to give the appearance that they participated in this 'magic exodus' casually. In spite of his own role within the rare book trade, Rosenbach described his relief at occasionally not being sold a book and noted admiringly how J. P. Morgan Sr. and his son avoided bidding against the British Museum when possible.[16] In practice, this seems to have involved arrangements not to bid on particular items until they reached sums that the Museum could not afford. Nonetheless, after a visit to Morgan's library, one English visitor admitted, 'I do not believe that any one in England knows how many things that ought never to have left the country are contained in these few cubic yards of space in New York,' adding sadly, 'I think that these heirlooms of England will never go back, and, I repeat, they should never have come here.'[17] It was important for both Morgan and his son to appear that they were safeguarding, rather than plundering, English cultural treasures – even if the results were the same.

Starting in 1890, Morgan Sr. collected a wide range of material until his death in 1913. At the end of his life *The New York Times* labelled him the 'Leading Collector of the Art World,' declaring that, 'it is safe to say that no American collector, however great his wealth, however impeccable his judgment, will ever be able to rival Mr. Morgan.'[18] Shortly after the Morgan Library's incorporation as an independent research library, a 1924 *New York Times* article put the value of the collection at $8.5 million, announcing: 'book lovers and collectors declare it the most magnificent gift of its kind ever made to the public.'[19] But it was a public gift with limitations as, 'one soiled thumb could undo the work of nine hundred years and a misplaced cough would be a disaster.'[20] Again, the emphasis here was on the Morgans' exceptional ability to preserve these items. At the same time, by celebrating Morgan Sr.'s private ownership while praising how he democratized book collecting, Morgan's reputation as a collector seems to dwarf the manuscripts themselves. This is an arrangement that would suit many American collectors – the collection being subsumed under the act of collecting.

As an American resident in Britain (who became a British citizen in 1933), Beatty fell into a slightly different category, not least because he was not exporting manuscripts from Britain in this period. Instead, he brought manuscripts into Britain from elsewhere in Europe and from America. For example, in 1920, on the advice of Sydney Cockerell, Beatty bought the de Brailes leaves (now in the Fitzwilliam Museum, Cambridge) from Dr. Rosenbach in New York, and returned with them to Britain.[21] Unlike Morgan Jr., Beatty did not inherit either a fortune or an art collection with an expert librarian, instead building his manuscript collection from scratch. However, in doing so he became part of the same small network of elite collectors, for example through membership of the Roxburghe Club, and engaged with the same small group of experts used by the Morgans and Greene. These included Cockerell and the keepers of manuscripts at the British Museum. In 1919, in response to a request from Greene, Dring recommended Sir George Warner, by then retired from the British Museum, as a potential cataloguer of the Morgans' manuscripts, or alternatively Cockerell, or M. R. James, whom Cockerell had succeeded at the Fitzwilliam, and who had taken up the Provostship of Eton

College. However, Dring noted that James was really interested in text, and Greene annotated the letter: 'yes and is utterly indifferent to the art side.'[22] Beatty later employed Eric G. Millar, then a keeper at the British Museum, to write the catalogue of his Western manuscripts.[23] In addition, Cockerell's diaries record his visits to many manuscript collections in the company of Beatty or Greene, as each developed their knowledge and connoisseurship through extensive study of books that would never come onto the market.[24] Cockerell recorded that on his first inspection of Beatty's nascent collection in 1915, he advised him to get rid of about half his collection of about 15 manuscripts.[25] Similarly, on his first visit to the Morgan Library, on a trip funded by Beatty, Cockerell spent one day 'looking through their inferior books which are numerous and ought to be got rid of,' although he also described the Library as 'a most beautiful building full of beautiful things.'[26]

The first authorized description of Morgan Sr.'s private library appeared on 4 December 1908 in both *The New York Times* and *The Times* of London.[27] In the article Morgan is characterized as a modern Medici with a thorough knowledge of the many objects he collected. However, as with several major American collectors, the size of Morgan's collection, and the pace with which it was assembled (Jean Strouse suggests that by 1912 Morgan had spent around $60 million on art) opens to question the full extent of Morgan's purported expertise.[28] In contrast, after Morgan Sr.'s death, Greene's correspondence reveals a highly critical judgement about what she deemed fit for the collection. When some of Beatty's manuscripts were put up for auction in 1932, Greene wrote to Ferguson declaring 'there are not many manuscripts in Mr. Millar's publication [i.e. of Beatty's collection] todate [sic] which I deem really important for our collection. But there are one or two which I would like to have if there is still a shilling left in the Library account.'[29] Greene's judgements were informed by financial constraints, though claims of poverty were also used to bargain with dealers, but her views were also driven by what was already in the collection.[30] When Greene really wanted something, money was not usually a problem. In advance of the Yates Thompson sale of 1919 she wrote to Dring, 'we *want* you to *buy* for us Martyrology – Monte C[a]ssino (lot 11), which you value at 1500. I had thought and hoped that we could get it for 1000 but it *must come here*.'[31] In a cable she gave Dring a commission bid for the volume of £3000, with the added instruction 'but buy.'[32] Quaritch secured the manuscript for £1600 (plus commission) together with three of the other four manuscripts and a printed book Greene wanted.[33]

The rhetoric about the exceptional quality of the Morgan collection was also employed by the Quaritch directors. In advance of the second sale of Beatty manuscripts in 1933, Ferguson wrote to Greene in response to a request for information about manuscripts that might be 'important' for the Library. He observed, 'Lot 41 is an interesting book, which may realise £1000 or so, but I expect you have similar or better,' to which a pencil note was added recording Greene's response: 'Have better (Cologne).'[34]

Despite Greene's dismissals, Beatty, following the example of Henry Yates Thompson, developed a reputation for only owning the highest quality material, although the criteria used in arriving at such judgements were rarely stated explicitly.[35] However, Beatty's collecting was concentrated in a much shorter period of time. At the 1919 Yates Thompson sale he was outbid, and it was only in the 1920s that he began to spend sums to rival the Morgan's purchases, before he decided to sell his Western manuscripts in 1932 in the wake of the Wall Street crash and subsequent economic crisis. Like Morgan and Greene, Beatty carefully assessed what he thought manuscripts ought to fetch on the market, though his wife Edith spent much larger sums on manuscripts bought as gifts for him.

While Morgan Sr. took seriously the advice given by Belle da Costa Greene regarding items entering and leaving the library, his son Jack would much more publicly accept Greene's expert guidance.[36] When the Earl of Leicester decided to sell four valuable manuscripts in 1926, Greene advised Morgan Jr. to handle the negotiations and purchasing personally.[37] After spending an estimated $500,000 Morgan later recalled, 'My librarian told me she wouldn't dare spend so much of my money. But, just the same, I wouldn't dare face her if I went home without the manuscripts.'[38] Thanks in part to Greene's influence, Morgan left his father's library mostly intact while at the same time giving 7,000 art objects to the Metropolitan Museum, donating 1,350 objects to the Wadsworth Atheneum in Hartford, permitting family members to keep paintings they especially liked, and selling other items to rival collectors.[39] Under Morgan Jr., the Morgan Library continued to purchase manuscripts in large numbers throughout the 1920s, though the economic crisis of the 1930s prompted caution. In December 1930 Greene wrote to Ferguson, 'it is not possible for Mr. Morgan to spend any considerable sum of money at this time [...]. *Confidentially* the situation in this country is more than serious, and it is an actual fact that every penny that can be spared must be used to feed and employ destitute people.'[40]

According to Rosenbach, what mattered was not expertise necessarily, but the collector's ability to buy and the business acumen that made such purchasing possible. In this, of course, he was flattering his clients. He declared it a 'wonderful and magnificent thing' that 'business kings' (like Morgan and Beatty) collected books.[41] Unlike academics, who made 'a sad mess' of the gathering of books, 'the instinct of the collector' allowed them to create remarkable collections even in cases where their understanding of the items in their possession was quite limited. For example, in the case of Henry E. Huntington, Rosenbach wrote: 'He was without doubt the greatest collector of books the world has ever known. Without possessing a profound knowledge of literature or of history, his flair for fine books was remarkable. His taste was sure, impeccable.'[42] That impeccable taste was shaped, in part, by Rosenbach's own guiding influence.

Alongside the involvement of professionals such as Rosenbach and Greene, timing made the Huntington and Morgan collections possible. In 1897 the U.S. government passed a law that levied a 20% import tax on works of art coming into the United States, with an exemption for books and manuscripts that were used for research, educational or cultural purposes. Because there were no financial penalties for buying a book in Europe and shipping it home, there was no excuse not to pursue desirable items wherever they might be. In addition, death duties in England prompted the dispersal of aristocratic collections.[43] And, finally, there was the issue of national pride: in the drive for the choicest books and manuscripts, American collectors were eager to bring the best items home. As Greene observed in a 1912 *New York Times* interview, all this book buying 'is a game with Mr. Morgan. And a very good one for America.'[44]

The London book trade

In addition to their debts to those working in museums, notably Greene, Cockerell and Millar, both Morgan Jr. and Beatty relied on dealers including Rosenbach and Bernard Quaritch Ltd. Quaritch offered books for sale through catalogues and bid on behalf of clients (including Beatty and the Morgan Library) at auctions, for which they charged commission. The First World War and the consequent disruption on the continent helped London to consolidate its position as a major centre for trade in books and manuscripts. In 1916 Dring informed Greene that, despite a decline in purchases from America, he had 'felt the war very much less than I anticipated. One thing it has certainly done, it has brought me into touch with universities and libraries in every quarter of the world with whom I have never before corresponded.'[45] The inclusion of such news in Dring's letters was one way in which he, and later Ferguson, developed and maintained relationships with their important international clients. Dring and Ferguson's knowledge of collectors' taste, interests and previous purchases enabled them to suggest volumes available for sale that were likely to be of interest.

Neither the Morgan Library nor Beatty dealt exclusively with Quaritch Ltd., and correspondence in the Morgan Library archives demonstrates that Greene was not averse to playing dealers off against each other. In

1930 Greene wrote to Ferguson stating: '*Most confidentially*, Dr Rosenbach thought this one in such bad condition that we ought not to retain it.'[46] To which Ferguson replied, 'It is all very well for Dr Rosenbach to think that it is in too bad a condition for you to keep, but he knows very well the rarity of the book.'[47] However, he also offered Greene a £25 discount on the volume. The long-running relationship and Quaritch's record-keeping could also work in the firm's favour. In 1932 Ferguson wrote to Greene in advance of the sale of part of Beatty's collection:

> In your letter you tell me that [...] there are not many MSS. to be offered in the forthcoming sale which you deem really important for the Morgan Library, but that you will be interested in one or two. I do not know whether one of these may be [...] the Mostyn Gospels, but I should like to recall the fact in the Mostyn Sale, where Beatty bought this MS. for £2550, you sent a commission of £2100, and cabled afterwards asking if this MS. could still be had.[48]

When Morgan eventually secured the Mostyn Gospels through Quaritch after the Beatty sale (for £2,000 plus commission), Ferguson wrote to congratulate Greene on the purchase, stating 'You have certainly secured a wonderful bargain, and I am sure you will be pleased with the book.'[49] To underline the value of his own role in the process, Ferguson continued, 'Before I cabled to you about it, I was asked to offer it to a man who has since told me he would paid a much larger sum than that for which you have bought it. However, I am very pleased that it will be in the Morgan Library.'

One of the challenges faced by dealers was keeping multiple clients who might be interested in the same items happy, whilst maintaining confidentiality. The Quaritch commission books demonstrate that at the Mostyn sale in 1920, in addition to holding rival bids from the Morgan Library, Beatty and Joseph Martini of New York for the Mostyn Gospels, Quaritch was also acting on behalf of clients including the British Museum. The latter lost out to Beatty on a Book of Hours (lot 63), but, most unusually, outbid the Morgan Library for another Gospel Book (now British Library, Add. MS 40000). Dring later wrote to Greene about the Mostyn sale, revealing that 'lot 39 was bought for the B[ritish] M[useum] and lot 40 by Mr Beatty. I gave you a very broad hint about the latter in my cable but could do no more as he had already consulted me about it.'[50] On other occasions Quaritch even bid on behalf of the Rosenbach Company.[51]

Correspondence between Beatty and Quaritch Ltd has yet to come to light, but the letters between Greene and both Dring and Ferguson often contain information that is identified as confidential. On the 30th of August 1918 Dring cabled Greene:

> CONFIDENTIAL YATES THOMPSONS MANUSCRIPTS ARE IN MARKET HE WRITES UNLESS OVERTEMPTED BY PR[I]VATE OFFER FIRST AUCTION WILL BE ANNOUNCED SOON WOULD YOU OFFER FOR WHOLE OR PREFER TO BUY INDIVIDUAL VOLUMES AT SALE HE IS VERY INDEPENDENT AND WILL NOT FIX PRICE.[52]

Dring thus gave Greene the option of trying to secure the whole collection, though Cockerell's diary indicates that the news of the sale had been made public that day.[53] When it became clear that Greene would not be able to come to England for the sale, Dring sent descriptions of some of the lots in the sale together with estimates of what they might fetch. It was in the run up to the first Yates Thompson sale in 1919 that Greene enquired about English collectors. Dring's response that there were half a dozen collectors prepared to pay £2,000–£3,000 for a volume is not supported by Quaritch's commission books, suggesting that Dring was talking up the potential prices, though Quaritch was, of course, not acting for all collectors. The first Yates Thompson sale was a notable success, and *The Times* reported that Quaritch was the largest single buyer, paying £41,680 of the total £52,360 raised.[54] Morgan was outbid for lot 5, the Hours of Jeanne II, Queen of Navarre, which Quaritch purchased for Baron Rothschild for £11,800 (plus commission).[55] However, in addition to the volumes bought by Morgan, Rothschild and the British Museum, only two other volumes appear to have sold for £2,000 or more. After the sale Dring wrote to Greene congratulating her on having got 'two or three great bargains' and offering her five volumes from those that had been bought for Quaritch's stock, on which the firm made an immediate profit.[56]

In 1927, the death of Sir George Holford raised the possibility that the famous library at Dorchester House might come onto the market.[57] Dring wrote to Greene, 'I can tell you confidentially that I personally with Mr Ferguson, valued the Library and the MSS. at Dorchester House for probate purposes, so I have a very good idea of what is there.'[58] Greene responded recommending that Quaritch buy the entire collection and adding, 'Please under no circumstances let the Executors know that I have spoken to you about the collection at all, and is there a possibility (without breaking a confidence) for you to give Mr Morgan and myself a general idea of the appraised value which as you can understand, would be helpful to us when the question comes up?'[59] Dring replied:

> I am quite sure that it would not be any guidance if I gave you an idea of the valuation [. . .]. It was purely for probate and both you and especially Mr. Morgan know quite well that when valuing for probate I place as small a value as I can on the various items.[60]

A minimal probate value helped to reduce the sums payable by the estate in death duties, demonstrating how Dring was seeking to serve both the seller and potential buyers. After the auction he revealed to Greene that he had valued the Holford miniatures (a collection of single leaves and excised illuminations) for probate at £7,500, and that they had made £10,100 at auction.[61] Both Beatty and the Morgan Library arranged private purchases from the executors, and Greene also sent bids for two items at the miniatures auction to Quaritch, observing 'I realize perfectly that you will use your discretion and get it for less if possible. // Of course this is just being played up for two people, Beatty and ourselves.'[62]

Among the purchases made by the Morgan Library from the Holford estate was the famous, extensively illuminated Life of Saint Edmund (now M. 736). This volume was mentioned repeatedly in the correspondence between Dring and Greene. In his first letter mentioning the valuation, Dring observed 'Naturally the British Museum want the St. Edmund MS. and I believe that there is a tacit understanding that when the collection is dispersed it shall go there for some agreed consideration.'[63] Greene replied, 'I quite agree with you that the British Museum should have the St. Edmund, and [. . .] in my opinion, the estate ought to arrange to practically give it to the British Museum.' However, she added 'of course we should want to acquire [it] if it is made impossible for the British Museum to do so.'[64] The manuscript was not in the group of five which were initially purchased by the Morgan Library, but was subsequently purchased from the executors.[65] A cryptic remark in a letter from Millar to Beatty seems to refer to the British Museum's attempt to secure the manuscript, and suggests that the executors were discussing 'a sum higher than the one we mentioned this afternoon, which is rather appalling.'[66] In a subsequent letter, Millar declared 'It is most disgusting about the St Edmund, and I can't feel that the executors have played the game with us.'[67] In a posthumous tribute to Greene, Sir Frederic Kenyon, Keeper at the British Museum, recalled that the manuscript was 'half-promise[d]' to the Museum at its probate valuation, but that the executors, presumably encouraged by the interest of at least two potential buyers including Morgan, subsequently demanded a price that the Museum could not pay. Nevertheless, he opined that Morgan and Greene had 'kept faith with the Museum.'[68]

The idea that certain manuscripts ought to remain in the modern equivalent of their country of origin was not only applied to British manuscripts.

After the 1919 Yates Thompson sale, Dring explained his failure to secure the Hours of Jeanne II, Queen of Navarre for the Morgan Library, accepting Rothschild's instructions to 'practically buy the volume coûte que coûte,' partly on the grounds that 'I bought it really to return it to France, where it really ought to be, and eventually it will most likely find its way into the Bibliothèque Nationale.'[69] Yet in 1903, concern about the departure of objects of historical and artistic significance from Britain had prompted the formation of the National Art-Collections Fund (NACF). In 1928, as part of an NACF publication, Sir Frederic Kenyon wrote a justification for retaining English manuscripts in their country of origin. He stated:

> it is important that illuminated manuscripts executed in England should be well represented, in order to drive home the fact, only recognized in recent years and still insufficiently realized, that throughout the medieval period [...] English painting always held a high, and often the highest, place in this branch of art.[70]

However, as demonstrated by the sale of the St Edmund manuscript, such considerations rarely weighed heavily with rich collectors or those keen to sell.

The problem of rich individuals being able to outbid museums led some keepers to work with private collectors in the hope of subsequently securing their treasures. In 1923 Cockerell identified a Book of Hours at Maggs Bros. that he wanted for the Fitzwilliam. He persuaded Beatty to buy it, and to stipulate that it should come to the museum after the death of himself and his wife.[71] In fact, Beatty gave it to the Museum in 1936. More famously, Morgan helped the British Museum to purchase the Luttrell Psalter and the Bedford Hours in 1929.[72] Both manuscripts had been deposited in the British Museum for over 20 years.[73] Any attempt by a private collector to purchase them would thus appear to be removing them from the 'national collection,' particularly if the books were sent abroad.[74] However, the Museum did not have unlimited funds with which to bid at auction. Eric Millar immediately asked both Beatty and Greene to 'resist any private offer of the books' and to persuade dealers including Rosenbach to do the same, trying to avoid a repeat of the Holford affair.[75] In his letter to Greene, Millar noted: 'you know the importance of the Loutterell [sic] Psalter as a national monument, and I am afraid that if it comes into a public auction it will have all the added publicity resulting from its deposit here.' In response Morgan offered to lend the British Museum whatever it cost to buy the manuscripts, which could be repaid, interest-free over the following year. If the Museum could not raise the money, the manuscripts would be his, as Millar described, secured 'absolutely and beyond all doubt for the Morgan Library.'[76] The absence of many of the likely bidders from the auction would also ensure that if Morgan obtained the manuscripts, he would get them at an excellent price. If unsuccessful in securing them for his own collection, he would be seen as the saviour of two of Britain's treasures. Quaritch was engaged to bid on the Museum's behalf, and offered to charge just 1% commission, instead of the usual 5% paid by the Museum and 10% paid by others. The subsequent circumstances of the auction had elements of both drama and farce, and Morgan's gamble nearly paid off, as in the wake of the Wall Street crash and economic crisis the British Museum struggled to raise the money.[77] However, in the end the appeal was successful, and a list of contributors was printed in the *British Museum Quarterly* and a volume written by Millar about the Luttrell Psalter.[78] Millar's book was dedicated to Morgan, and among the list of the largest donations were the names of other private collectors, including Mr. Dyson Perrins, Beatty and Mr. Gulbenkian, all keen to be associated with this famous effort to save a book for the nation, though contributing less than they spent on many volumes for their own libraries.

The interwar period, particularly before 1929, was a golden age for the trade in illuminated manuscripts in London. The boom in prices was fuelled, in part, by American collectors, foremost amongst whom was the Morgan Library. This, in turn, contributed to concerns about the export of books, some of which were described as 'national monuments.' At the same time, American collectors were carefully cultivated by dealers, and admitted to the small circle of British collectors and scholars. Collectors valued the knowledge and connoisseurship of scholars, and the museum-based experts (notably Sydney Cockerell) in turn sought to persuade collectors to enrich museums in Britain and to sponsor publications. The demand for information about books also led to increasingly extensive descriptions in many dealer and auction catalogues. These tensions reached a peak with the sale of the Luttrell Psalter and Bedford Hours in 1929, immediately before the start of the Great Depression. The connections of staff at the British Museum enabled them to attempt to manipulate the market, at the same time calling on public opinion to preserve the 'treasures' in the Museum. J. P. Morgan's gamble was a clever one. In losing the manuscripts he gained a reputation that made it difficult to oppose his many other purchases. In the same way, the generous, large donations by those who had also abstained from bidding for the manuscripts, and Quaritch's minimal commission, may have been prompted, in part, by a desire to obtain similar approbation as they continued to build private collections, from the public, but also from those involved in the manuscript trade.

Notes

The research for this paper was made possible, in part, by an Irish Research Council New Foundations Grant, and the authors are very grateful for this support. In addition, they would like to thank the staff of the Morgan Library, Bernard Quaritch Ltd. and the Chester Beatty Library for access to their archives.

1 New York, Morgan Library Archive, ARC 1310 Q, Quaritch VI 1918/19.
2 On Belle da Costa Greene see Dorothy Miner, 'Foreword,' in *Studies in Art and Literature for Belle da Costa Greene*, ed. by Dorothy Miner (Princeton: Princeton University Press, 1954), pp. ix–xiii; Heidi Ardizzone, *An Illuminated Life: Belle da Costa Greene's Journey from Prejudice to Privilege* (New York: W. W. Norton & Company, 2007).
3 Ardizzone, *An Illuminated Life*, pp. 380–381.
4 Letter from Greene to Dring, 22 June 1919, New York, Morgan Library Archive, ARC 1310 Q, Quaritch VI 1918/19.
5 Letter from Dring to Greene, 17 July 1919, Morgan Library Archive, ARC 1310 Q, Quaritch VI 1918/19; Edmund M. Dring, 'Fifty Years at Quaritch,' *The Book Collector: Special Number for the 150th Anniversary of Bernard Quaritch* (1997), 35–52 (at p. 38).
6 Arthur J. Wilson, *The Life & Times of Sir Alfred Chester Beatty* (London: Cadogan Publications, 1985), p. 136.
7 Sydney Carlyle Cockerell, 'Diary for 1919,' British Library, Add. MS 52656 f. 25v, entry for 4 June. On Cockerell see: Christopher de Hamel, *Hidden Friends: A Loan Exhibition of the Comites Latentes Collection of Illuminated Manuscripts from the Bibliothèque Publique et Universitaire, Geneva* (London: Sotheby & Co, 1985); Christopher de Hamel, 'Medieval and Renaissance Manuscripts from the Library of Sir Sydney Cockerell,' *The British Library Journal* (1987), 186–210; Christopher de Hamel, 'Cockerell as Entrepreneur,' *The Book Collector*, 55 (2006), 49–72; Christopher de Hamel, 'Cockerell as Museum Director,' *The Book Collector*, 55 (2006), 201–223; Christopher de Hamel, 'Cockerell as Collector,' *The Book Collector*, 55 (2006), 339–366; S. Panayotova, *I Turned it into a Palace: Sydney Cockerell and the Fitzwilliam Museum* (Cambridge: Fitzwilliam Museum, 2008). See also Stella Panayotova's essay in this volume.
8 Letter from Dring to Greene, 11 June 1919, Morgan Library Archive, ARC 1310 Q, Quaritch VI 1918/19.
9 Abraham S. W. Rosenbach, 'Why America Buys England's Books,' *The Atlantic Monthly* (October, 1927), 452–459 (at 454). On Rosenbach see: E. Wolf and J. F. Fleming, *Rosenbach: A Biography* (London: Weidenfeld and Nicolson, 1960).
10 'Some Recent Phases of Book Collecting,' *The Times* (26 December 1906), 6.
11 'Topics of the Week,' *The New York Times* (31 March 1906), 196.
12 Rosenbach, 'Why America Buys,' 453.
13 *Ibid.*, 454.
14 *Ibid.*, 459.
15 See A. N. L. Munby and L. W. Tower, *The Flow of Books and Manuscripts* (Los Angeles: William Andrews Clark Memorial Library, 1969), p. 8.
16 Rosenbach, 'Why America Buys,' 453, 458.
17 'Mr. Morgan's Great Library,' *The New York Times* (4 December 1908), 2.

18 'Leading Collector of the Art World,' *The New York Times* (1 April 1913), 5.
19 'J. P. Morgan Gives Library to the Public,' *The New York Times* (17 February 1924), 1; see also *The Pierpont Morgan Library: A Review of the Growth, Development and Activities of the Library during the Period between Its Establishment as an Educational Institution in February 1924 and the Close of the Year 1929* (New York: Pierpont Morgan Library, 1930).
20 'J. P. Morgan Gives Library to the Public,' 14.
21 Sydney Carlyle Cockerell, 'Diary for 1920,' British Library Add. MS 52657, f. 53v; Sydney Carlyle Cockerell, *The Work of W. de Brailes: An English Illuminator of the Thirteenth Century* (Cambridge: Cambridge University Press, 1930); see also Christopher de Hamel, 'Cockerell as Museum Director,' 215, 217.
22 Letter from E. H. Dring to Greene, 17 July 1919, Morgan Library Archive, ARC 1310 Q, Quaritch VI 1918/19.
23 Eric George Millar, *The Library of A. Chester Beatty: A Descriptive Catalogue of the Western Manuscripts*, 2 vols. (Oxford: Oxford University Press, 1927–1930). See L. Cleaver, 'The Western Manuscript Collection of Alfred Chester Beatty (ca. 1915–1930),' *Manuscript Studies*, 2.2 (2017), 445–482.
24 Cockerell first met Greene in 1908 when they visited libraries in Cambridge: Sydney Carlyle Cockerell, 'Diary for 1908,' British Library Add. MS 52645, f. 66v; Ardizzone, *An Illuminated Life*, p. 380.
25 Sydney Carlyle Cockerell, 'Diary for 1915,' British Library Add. MS 53652, f. 59.
26 Sydney Carlyle Cockerell, 'Diary for 1920,' British Library, Add. MS 52657, f. 52v.
27 'Mr Morgan's Great Library,' p. 1; 'Mr. Pierpont Morgan's Library,' *The Times* (4 December 1908), 12.
28 Jean Strouse, *Morgan: American Financier* (New York: Random House Books, 1999), p. 7.
29 Letter from Greene to Ferguson, 21 April 1932, Morgan Library Archive, ARC 1310 Q, Quaritch X, 1930–32.
30 See also Lawrence C. Wroth, 'A Tribute to the Library and Its First Director,' *The First Quarter Century of the Pierpont Morgan Library* (New York: Pierpont Morgan Library, 1949), pp. 14–15.
31 Letter from Greene to Dring, 13 May 1919, Morgan Library Archive, ARC 1310 Q, Quaritch VI 1918/19.
32 Cable from Morgan Library to Quaritch Ltd, 26 May 1919, Morgan Library Archive, ARC 1310 Q, Quaritch VI 1918/19.
33 Quaritch Archive, Commission Book for 1917–20, p. 1353; the manuscripts are now Morgan Library MSS M. 639, M. 641, M. 642, M. 644. After the sale the Morgan Library also purchased two further items from Quaritch, which are now M. 640 and M. 643. See also letter from Dring to Greene, 4 June 1919, Morgan Library Archive, ARC 1310 Q, Quaritch VI 1918/19.
34 Letter from Ferguson to Greene, 11 April 1933, Morgan Library Archive, ARC 1310 Q, Quaritch XI, 1933–36.
35 See Cleaver, 'The Western Manuscript Collection.'
36 Ardizzone, *An Illuminated Life*, pp. 366–370.
37 The manuscripts are now Morgan Library, MSS M. 708–11.
38 Wroth, p. 19; see also F. G. Kenyon, 'A Tribute from the British Museum,' in *Studies in Art and Literature for Belle da Costa Greene*, ed. by D. Miner (Princeton: Princeton University Press, 1954), pp. 4–5.

39 Figures from Metmuseum.org and thewadsworth.org. See also Rachel Cohen, 'J. P. Morgan: The Man Who Bought the World,' *Apollo*, 5 September 2015, <www.apollo-magazine.com/j-p-morgan-the-man-who-bought-the-world/>; (accessed 12 January 2018).
40 Letter from Greene to Ferguson, 12 December 1930, Morgan Library Archive, ARC 1310 Q, Quaritch X, 1930–32.
41 Rosenbach, 'Why America Buys,' 456.
42 *Ibid.*, 455.
43 Dugald Sutherland Maccoll, *Twenty-Five Years of the National Art-Collections Fund 1903–1928* (Glasgow: National Art-Collections Fund, 1928), p. 4.
44 'Spending J. P. Morgan's Money for Rare Books,' *The New York Times* (7 April 1912), 1.
45 Letter from Dring to Greene, 24 January 1916, Morgan Library Archive, ARC 1310 Q, Quaritch V, 1915–17.
46 Letter from Greene to Ferguson, 8 October 1930, Morgan Library Archive, ARC 1310 Q, Quaritch X 1930–32.
47 Letter from Ferguson to Greene, 12 December 1930, Morgan Library Archive, ARC 1310 Q, Quaritch X 1930–32.
48 Letter from Ferguson to Greene, 13 May 1932, Morgan Library Archive, ARC 1310 Q, Quaritch X 1930–32.
49 Letter from Ferguson to Greene, 10 June 1930, Morgan Library Archive, ARC 1310 Q, Quaritch X 1930–32.
50 Letter from Dring to Greene, 15 April 1920, Morgan Library Archive, ARC 1310 Q, Quaritch VII 1920–22.
51 See also Wolf and Fleming, *Rosenbach*, pp. 60–61.
52 Cable from Quaritch Ltd to Morgan Library, 5 January 1918, Morgan Library Archive, ARC 1310 Q, Quaritch VI 1918/19.
53 Sydney Carlyle Cockerell, 'Diary for 1918,' British Library, Add. MS 52655 f. 49.
54 'Yates Thompson MSS,' *The Times* (4 June 1919), 14.
55 Quaritch Archives Commission Book for 1917–20, p. 1353.
56 Letter from Dring to Greene, 11 June 1919, Morgan Library Archive, ARC 1310 Q, Quaritch VI 1918/19.
57 See also Leslie A. Morris, *Rosenbach Abroad: In Pursuit of Books in Private Collections* (Philadelphia: Rosenbach Museum and Library, 1988).
58 Letter from Dring to Greene, 3 May 1927, Morgan Library Archive, ARC 1310 Q, Quaritch IX 1927–29.
59 Letter from Greene to Dring, 12 May 1927, Morgan Library Archive, ARC 1310 Q, Quaritch IX 1927–29.
60 Letter from Dring to Greene, 27 May 1927, Morgan Library Archive, ARC 1310 Q, Quaritch IX 1927–29.
61 Letter from Dring to Greene, 12 July 1927, Morgan Library Archive, ARC 1310 Q, Quaritch IX 1927–29; see also 'The Sale Room,' *The Times* (13 July 1927), 10.
62 Letter from Greene to Dring, 29 June 1927, Morgan Library Archive, ARC 1310 Q, Quaritch IX 1927–29; the leaves are now Morgan Library, M. 724 and M. 725.
63 Letter from Dring to Greene, 3 May 1927, Morgan Library Archive, ARC 1310 Q, Quaritch IX 1927–29.
64 Letter from Greene to Dring, 12 May 1927, Morgan Library Archive, ARC 1310 Q, Quaritch IX 1927–29.

65 These are now Morgan Library, MSS M. 728–32.
66 Letter from Millar to Beatty, 7 December 1927, Chester Beatty Library Archive, Millar Correspondence.
67 Letter from Millar to Beatty, 5 January 1928, Chester Beatty Library Archive, Millar Correspondence.
68 Kenyon, 'A Tribute from the British Museum,' p. 5.
69 Letter from Dring to Greene, 11 June 1919, Morgan Library Archive, ARC 1310 Q, Quaritch VI, 1918/19. The manuscript is now Paris, Bibliothèque nationale de France, MS nouv. acq. lat 3145, but its acquisition was much less straightforward than Dring could have foreseen; see Christopher de Hamel, *The Rothschilds and Their Collections of Illuminated Manuscripts* (London: British Library, 2005), p. 41; Christopher de Hamel, *Meetings with Remarkable Manuscripts* (London: Allen Lane, 2016), pp. 376–425.
70 *Twenty-Five Years of the National Art-Collections Fund*, pp. 201–202.
71 Cockerell, 'Diary for 1923,' British Library, Add. MS 52660, f. 45v; see also Panayotova, *I Turned It into a Palace*, p. 156.
72 Janet Backhouse, 'The Sale of the Luttrell Psalter,' in *Antiquaries, Book Collectors and the Circles of Learning* (Winchester: St Paul's Bibliographies, 1996), pp. 113–128.
73 *Ibid*., p. 114.
74 Letter from Ferguson to Greene, 2 July 1929, British Library, Add. MS 74095.
75 Letter from Millar to Greene, 8 January 1929, British Library, Add. MS 74095; see also Backhouse, 'The Sale of the Luttrell Psalter,' p. 118.
76 Letter from Millar to H. Idris Bell, 26 July 1929, British Library, Add. MS 74095; see also Backhouse, 'The Sale of the Luttrell Psalter,' p. 120.
77 See Backhouse, 'The Sale of the Luttrell Psalter.'
78 Eric George Millar, *The Luttrell Psalter* (London: British Museum, 1932).

6 Sydney Cockerell

A bibliophile director-collector

Stella Panayotova

Confined to bed, the octogenarian Cockerell (1867–1962) re-read and annotated the extensive series of diaries that he had kept throughout his life. He captioned the entry for 30 May 1908 'ELECTED DIRECTOR OF THE FITZWILLIAM and a new chapter of my life lasting nearly 30 years about to begin.'[1] This chapter ended in 1937, when he retired at the age of 70 (see Figure 6.1). The longest ruling and most acquisitive Fitzwilliam Director to date, Cockerell made a lasting impact on art institutions in the UK, the United States and Australia.[2]

A disciple and friend of John Ruskin and William Morris, associated with the Arts and Crafts Movement, Cockerell was a major figure in London's artistic and literary circles during the decades on either side of 1900.[3] He rubbed shoulders with artists, writers, scholars and collectors: Edward Burne-Jones, George Bernard Shaw, Montague Rhodes James, Henry Yates Thomson and Roger Fry, to name but a few. These men in turn introduced him – or he introduced himself – to other luminaries in the world of art and letters, notably Thomas Hardy, Henry James, Swinburne, Yeats, Galsworthy, Tolstoy, Chekhov, Rudyard Kipling, Ezra Pound, Sargent, Sickert, Alec Guinness and Vanessa Redgrave.

Cockerell had an impressive portfolio of skills, including the running of a book dealer's shop and a typographic design business, and the roles of advisor and executor of formidable collectors in the early twentieth century. He combined academic expertise with administrative acumen and intimate knowledge of the art market.[4] Cockerell's reputation as a museum director was due – and still is – to his ambitious acquisitions, building campaigns and innovative approach to display.[5] When he arrived at the Fitzwilliam in 1908, he found a 'jumbled,' 'barbarous,' 'complete and repellent muddle' of all periods and styles, a dark, overcrowded cabinet of curiosities reserved for university dons who rarely visited.[6] Cockerell transformed it into a 'palace' of the arts and, despite much

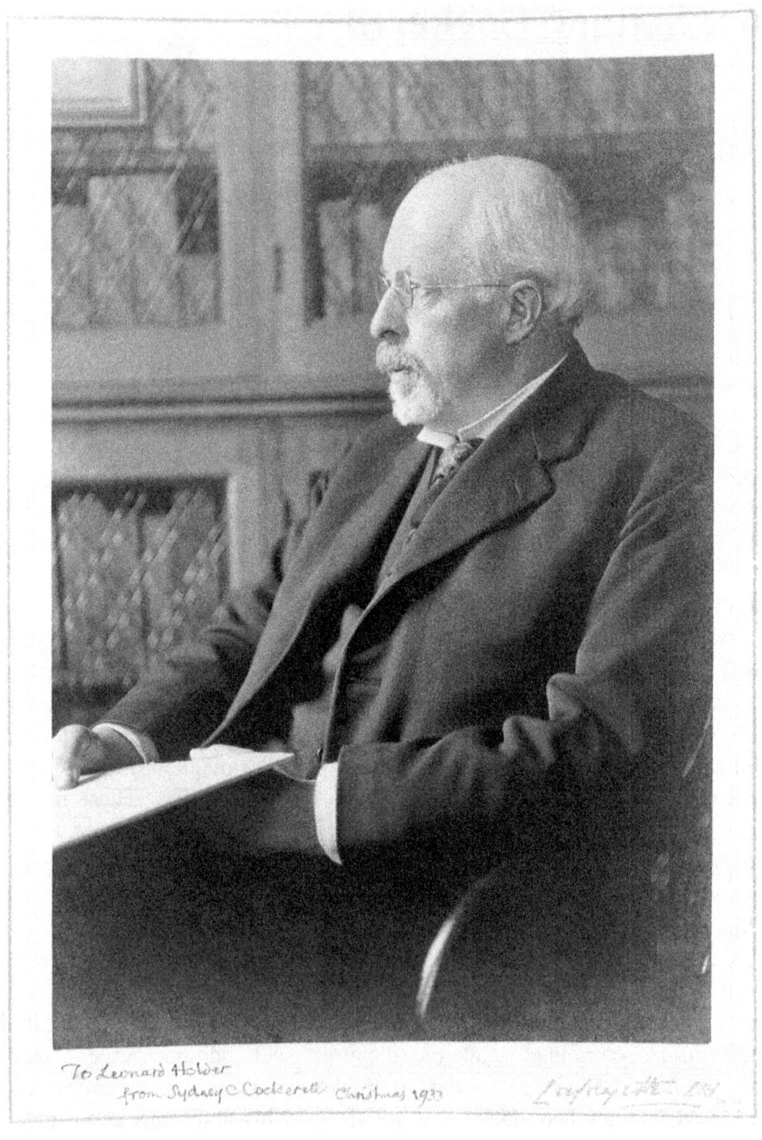

Figure 6.1 Sydney Cockerell in the Manuscripts Room, Fitzwilliam Museum, 1933

Fitzwilliam Museum, PH 1–1991 (© The Fitzwilliam Museum)

opposition, opened it to the public.[7] He added 17 new galleries and study rooms, doubling the size of the original building.[8]

He built his first extension in the 1920s with the bequest of Charles Brinsley Marlay. Upon his death in 1912, the Fitzwilliam received Marlay's vast and eclectic collection as well as £100,000, allowing Cockerell to launch his first building campaign and to establish a much-needed purchase fund.[9] Marlay's taste for the exotic and mentality of 'a bargain-hunter' (in Cockerell's words) marred his collection with second-rate objects and some of dubious authenticity. Cockerell persuaded the Duke of Rutland, Marlay's nephew and executor, to authorize the sale of anything that the Director considered to be 'modern, imitation, or of too low standard for an important museum.'[10] The disposals provoked criticism, but created a substantial fund for acquisitions. Although the new purchases were supposed to match the benefactor's interests, they ranged across Greek vases, Assyrian antiquities, Old Master prints, Pre-Raphaelite paintings, Elizabethan music and illuminated manuscripts, filling gaps in the Museum's holdings or inaugurating new collections.

Cockerell's treatment of the Marlay bequest was the first demonstration of his astute acquisitions policy. When subsequent donations or bequests were offered, he insisted that they should be accompanied by funds for the care, display and further growth of the collections. He also reserved the right to make a selection, to sell unwanted objects and to use the proceeds for new acquisitions. Cockerell employed a mirror reflection of the Marlay bequest strategy to his second major building-*cum*-acquisitions campaign. The new wing which opened in 1931 was financed by members of the Courtauld family, who had made a fortune in the nineteenth-century silk industry. The Director knew this from the press and from Lord Lee of Fareham. Cockerell visited Samuel Courtauld, the Chairman of the firm's Directors, whose home on Portman Square housed the most important collection of Impressionist art in Britain and hosted the famous Courtauld-Sargent concerts. Courtauld declined; he was committed to the National Gallery and was soon to finance Lord Lee's foundation of the Courtauld Institute.

Cockerell pursued other Courtaulds who had studied at Cambridge: William, his brother Stephen and their sister Miss Sydney René Courtauld. Newspaper cuttings and lists of names with addresses preserved among Cockerell's files reveal his research on the Courtaulds.[11] In June 1925 he wrote to them with the estimate for the new wing, £100,000, and over the next few years urged the siblings to compete with one another until the full sum was raised. He also extracted donations from Miss Courtauld for high-profile acquisitions, including ancient jewellery bought at the Hermitage sale in 1931 and Tintoretto's *Adoration of the Shepherds* purchased from the Countess of Suffolk in 1932.[12]

Cockerell pioneered a mixed-media display modelled on grand country houses. Combining paintings, furniture, tapestries, sculpture, musical instruments, ceramics and carpets, he created an opulent and welcoming period style in each gallery, offering an educational journey through time.[13] The success prompted one of his famous statements: ‘I found it a pigsty; I turned it into a palace.’[14]

Cockerell’s novel approach to display and lighting transformed the Fitzwilliam into a model for art institutions from Birmingham and London to West Carolina and Melbourne.[15] Martin Hardie, Keeper of Paintings, Drawings and Prints at the Victoria and Albert Museum, was among the guests at the opening of the new Courtauld wing on 5 June 1931. The next day, he wrote to Cockerell: ‘Your new galleries – and your collections – are wonderful. I feel the Victoria and Albert Museum should be pulled down and reconstructed.’[16] On Sunday, 29 May 1932, Kenneth Clark toured the Fitzwilliam, Cockerell’s diary tells us, and ‘was astonished at the number of visitors (we had 355 in the course of the afternoon) as there had only been 16 at the Ashmolean last Sunday!’[17]

If the Museum’s space was doubled, the collections were trebled. Cockerell’s fame today rests largely on the insatiable appetite and determination with which he amassed treasures for the Fitzwilliam. His diaries and letters contain enough self-congratulatory comments to justify the anecdotes that circulated about him. Among them is a College don’s report of the first words he heard Sydney Cockerell utter: ‘So I called on the duke: he was a dying man then.’[18] Receiving a note in Cockerell’s hand, the Duke of Devonshire sighed: ‘I must be dead.’ The Director regaled the Museum Syndics with stories about his latest spoils. While doodling on the agenda for a meeting in 1934, a Syndic summed up Cockerell’s tales in a sketch labelled ‘St Cockerellius relieving a poor traveller of a manuscript’ (Figure 6.2). Upon Cockerell’s retirement, the Chancellor of the University stated in his speech that ‘no collector in the world’ thought his treasures safe ‘so long as Sir Sydney is in the land.’[19] Years after his retirement, Cockerell continued to instruct his successor on dealing with donors: ‘Unconditional surrender should be the rule in every case.’[20]

Anecdotes aside, Cockerell’s strategy as a Director-Collector was both complex and flexible. We saw one of his approaches – the coupling of building campaigns with the establishment of purchase funds. Let us consider his other stratagems, using book acquisitions as examples.[21] The two most important things in Cockerell’s life were books and friendships.[22] His books forged and nurtured friendships; his friendships led to the acquisitions of books. His top priority, expertise and passion lay with illuminated manuscripts.

On 5 June 1908, less than a week after the announcement of his appointment to the Fitzwilliam Directorship and two weeks before taking up the

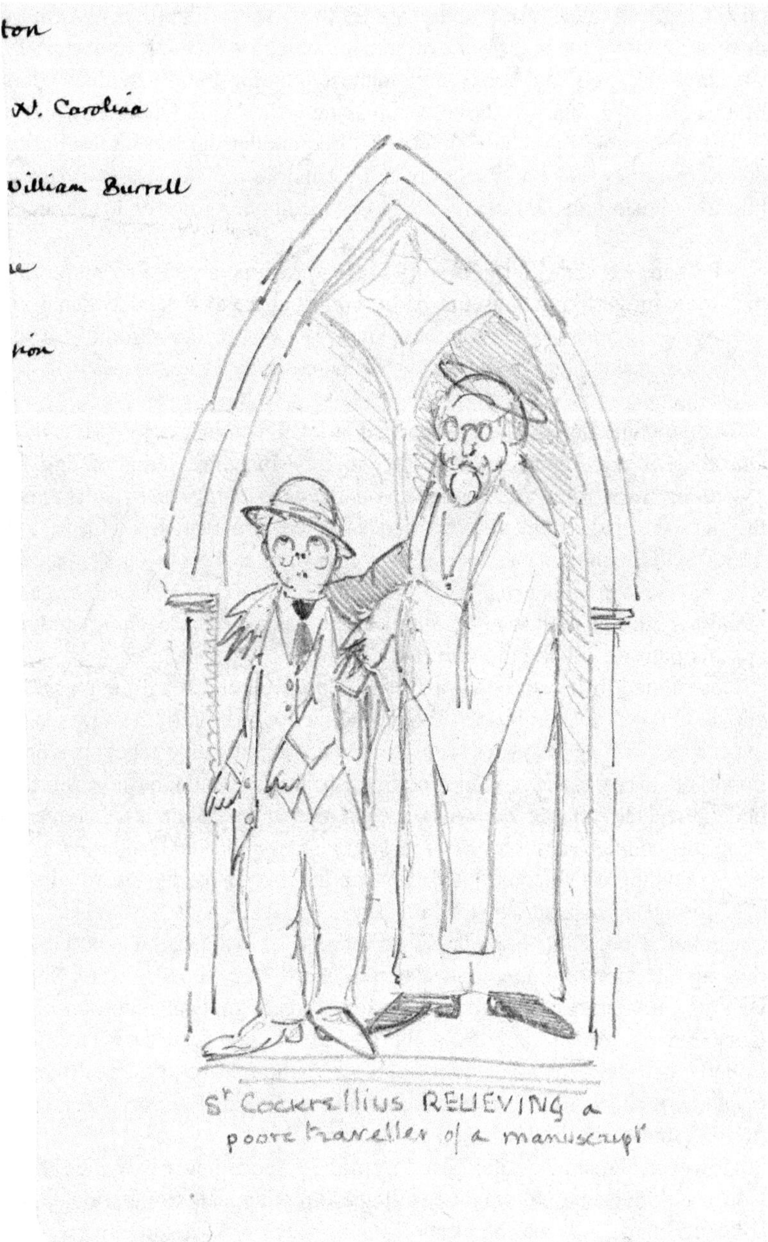

Figure 6.2 Sir Clive Forster Cooper, *St Cockerellius relieving a poor traveller of a manuscript*, 1934

Fitzwilliam Museum, MS 788–1991 (© The Fitzwilliam Museum)

post, Cockerell made his first purchase for the Museum: a thirteenth-century manuscript of *Pictor in Carmine* offered at Sotheby's.[23] By November 1908, Cockerell was buying books and manuscripts for the Fitzwilliam from Maggs and by January 1909 he was placing orders with Quaritch.

The slim annual purchase fund of £50 compelled him to trade his academic expertise and knowledge of the art market. When dealers thanked him for advising on their manuscripts, Cockerell put a price on his services:

> Perhaps Mr Charles Davis would care to recompense me by presenting something to this Museum or by contributing to a fund which I am trying to raise for the purchase of works of art, our resources being totally inadequate in these days of increasingly large prices.[24]

The new fund that Cockerell launched in 1909, within a year of his arrival, was that of the Friends of the Fitzwilliam Museum.[25] Epitomizing his regard for friendship and modelled on the *Societé des amis de Louvre*, this was the first group of supporters founded at a British art institution. The Friends' annual subscriptions created a fund at the Director's disposal with no strings attached. While recruiting Friends, Cockerell targeted mainly wealthy Cambridge *alumni*, but he was also approaching students and his patrons outside the university.

Determined to recruit on a vast scale, Cockerell contacted the press. On 15 March 1909, the *Daily Mail* announced the foundation of the new society in an article which resonates with Cockerell's pontificating tone: 'It is very important that the finest works of English artists should be accessible to undergraduates and even dons, who are apt to imagine that art is a Continental thing for the long vacation.' Both undergraduates and 'Old Cambridge men' who 'may appreciate some link other than cricket or rowing' were advised that 'fortunate coups at Newmarket should also result in benefactions.'

Cockerell used the Friends' subscriptions for wide-ranging purchases. Among the first illuminations acquired with their support were Simon Bening's miniatures from the Hours of Albrecht of Brandenburg, which Cockerell bought in 1918 from the son of the late Rev. Dewick.[26] The Friends also paid for manuscripts and leaves bought on the open market: from Quaritch in 1911, from Frank Sabin in 1915 and 1916, from Sotheby's in 1932 and from the Robinson brothers in 1935.[27]

However, the annual total raised from the Friends never exceeded £300. Cockerell devised an alternative strategy: direct appeals to individuals. He solicited loans, gifts and bequests from his friends in artistic, literary, aristocratic, political and business circles, and from the major collectors among his earlier patrons and employers. The earliest acquisitions honoured his two mentors: John Ruskin and William Morris.

Tours with Ruskin around French cathedrals and visits to his home at Brantwood had established Cockerell's lifelong passion for Gothic art and taste for Turner. During his last visit to the dying Ruskin in 1899, Cockerell examined 'the wonderful St Louis Psalter.'[28] Ruskin had bought the manuscript in 1854, recording in his diary: 'I got the greatest treasure in all my life: St Louis' Psalter.'[29] He had cut out leaves to use as teaching tools in Oxford or as gifts; in 1861 he sent three leaves to Professor Charles Eliot Norton in Harvard with the promise: 'If they sink on the way, I will send two others.'[30] A few years later, Cockerell would reassemble the dispersed leaves and the manuscript would become what he considered his finest acquisition for the Fitzwilliam.

It was another manuscript that occasioned Cockerell's first visit to Cambridge and epitomized his relationship with his next hero, William Morris. On 22 October 1896, Cockerell delivered to the Fitzwilliam the fourteenth-century Pabenham-Clifford Hours.[31] Morris had bought it at the Fountaine sale at Christie's in July 1894 for £410 and shown it to his friends. One of them, the typographer, printer and designer Emery Walker, recognized that two leaves were missing: they were at the Fitzwilliam. Walker was providing the images for the catalogue of the Museum's manuscripts about to be published by the then Director, M. R. James. After complex negotiations, Morris and James struck a deal.[32] The Museum gave Morris £200 and the two leaves so that he could enjoy them for the rest of his life; after that the volume was to come to the Fitzwilliam. Three weeks after Morris's death, Cockerell brought the Hours to Cambridge.

William Morris's command over a vast range of fine and decorative arts had exerted a profound impact on Cockerell's taste. Most decisive was his involvement with Morris's library which grew on an unprecedented scale in the 1890s, the last decade of Morris's life and the one devoted to his last great enterprise, the Kelmscott Press. In 1892 Cockerell began cataloguing the library and purchasing manuscripts. He accompanied Morris to private collections and auction rooms, sharpening his negotiation skills and expanding his knowledge of the book trade. In 1894 Cockerell was promoted from Morris's librarian to Secretary of the Kelmscott Press. By then, he had become indispensable to Morris, his family and his circle. The latter included Burne-Jones, Charles Fairfax Murray, George Bernard Shaw, Cobden-Sanderson and Emery Walker (who would become Cockerell's closest friend).

After Morris's death, Cockerell took care of his widow and daughters. The families of Morris and Burne-Jones introduced him to other important figures in the world of arts, literature, music and politics, notably Stanley Baldwin (who would champion Cockerell's Knighthood), Yeats, Oscar Wilde, Rudyard Kipling, Roger Fry, Bernard Berenson and the artists-connoisseurs-collectors Charles Ricketts and Charles Shannon. Two of the acquaintances that Cockerell made at Kelmscott House determined his future. From 1899, he divided his time evenly between his two new employers: Wilfrid Blunt and Henry Yates Thompson.[33]

Wilfrid Blunt, a wealthy landowner and former diplomat, was by 1900 a sworn anti-imperialist, self-taught Arabist, passionate horse-breeder, poet and philanderer. Blunt was married to Byron's granddaughter, Lady Anne, who was to his chagrin a better Arabist and horse-breeder than him. Through Blunt and Lady Anne, Cockerell developed an interest in the literature and arts of the Orient. While staying at their house outside Cairo, he visited Karnak, Luxor, Sakkara, Memphis and Damascus, marvelling at the pyramids, the sphinx, mosques and manuscripts. As Blunt's secretary and executor, Cockerell was a regular guest at the aristocracy's fashionable country houses which would provide models for the new interiors in his future Museum.

Henry Yates Thompson, the eldest son of a Liverpool banker, had inherited a library from his grandfather, the antiquarian Joseph Brooks Yates, but by 1892 he was building his own collection of illuminated manuscripts. Upon Morris's death in 1896, he visited Kelmscott House to negotiate purchases, but was too late.[34] In 1898 Yates Thompson bought some 210 manuscripts from the Library of the Earl of Ashburnham, but soon after decided to own only one hundred of the finest manuscripts at any time. He needed help with the cataloguing and weeding out of manuscripts, and Cockerell joined M. R. James in researching, selling and buying manuscripts for Yates Thompson. The quality control that he had to exercise raised his standards. Later, at the Fitzwilliam, he would confess: 'I often wished I'd got a machine-gun mounted at the top of the stairs to mow down the people who tried to make me accept second-rate and third-rate objects.'[35]

The acquisitions made in 1909, Cockerell's first full year in Cambridge, reveal that his initial point of call was his immediate circle of friends and collectors: Wilfrid Blunt, Henry Yates Thompson, Charles Fairfax Murray and the families of William Morris and Burne-Jones. Wilfrid Blunt offered the original manuscript of his poem *Esther*, laying the foundations of a new collection – literary autographs. Lady Burne-Jones presented the manuscript of the *Icelandic Sagas* copied and illuminated for her by William Morris. Exemplifying one of Morris's many endeavours, this was the start of another new collection – modern calligraphy and illumination. The Director was particularly keen on it, since he had promoted the careers of talented calligraphers, notably Edward Johnston, Graily Hewitt and his own wife, Florence Kate Kingsford.[36]

In 1909 Morris's widow donated the Kelmscott Press edition of Morris's poems, *The Earthly Paradise*, and Cockerell inaugurated yet another new collection – Private Press books.[37] The Fitzwilliam Director was the living link between Morris's revival of fine printing and the next generation of typographers and designers that established the leading English Private Presses. Through his friendship with their founders he secured their finest editions for his Museum. Ricketts and Shannon offered the books of their Vale Press. Emery Walker and Cobden-Sanderson gave editions of their Doves Press, including the Doves Bible with an initial penned by Edward Johnston. In 1909, St John Hornby offered the crowning achievement of his Ashendene Press: 'his magnificent folio Dante,' Cockerell reported, 'which competes with the Kelmscott Chaucer as the finest printed book of modern times.'[38] It was the Kelmscott Chaucer that the Director coveted most. In 1930 Morris's daughter Jenny lent the Chaucer together with her entire set of Kelmscott books. Upon her death in 1935 she bequeathed them to the Fitzwilliam.

One of Cockerell's stratagems was to negotiate loans and transform them into gifts or bequests. In 1932 he secured John Keats's autograph of *An Ode to a Nightingale* on loan from the Marquess of Crewe.[39] A year later the Marquess asked to have it back, but Cockerell persuaded him to donate it instead.

As well as relying on existing benefactors, Cockerell cultivated new ones, starting with members of the university. For those who had no existing connection with Cambridge, he created a new one. Among his most willing victims was Thomas Hardy. Cockerell had neither met Hardy nor read any of his works when he wrote to him in 1911, asking for autographs. He was invited for a visit and within two hours extracted the manuscripts of *Jude the Obscure* and *Times' Laughingstock.* He wasted no time in creating the missing Cambridge link: in 1913 he secured for Hardy an honorary degree from the university to which the writer had dreamed of applying as a young man, an aspiration echoed in *Jude the Obscure.*

The only collector who claimed Cockerell's time and expertise on a par with Yates Thompson from 1904 onwards was Charles William Dyson Perrins who had turned his wealth inherited from the Lea & Perrins Worcester sauce into Royal Worcestershire porcelain and illuminated manuscripts.[40] As with Thompson, Cockerell was both building and researching Dyson Perrins's collection. While in Paris in 1906, they bought a thirteenth-century Book of Hours signed by the Oxford illuminator William de Brailes,[41] an artist who would play an important role in Cockerell's scholarship and later acquisitions.

Cockerell never finished the catalogue of Dyson Perrins's manuscripts. When George Warner completed it in 1920, after his retirement from the British Museum, he acknowledged Cockerell's contribution and expressed regret that it could not have been greater due to the onerous duties of the

Fitzwilliam Directorship. Cockerell did not have time to catalogue the Fitzwilliam's manuscripts either; he was too busy acquiring them. But there may have been other reasons for his modest involvement in Dyson Perrins's catalogue. Cockerell worked on Yates Thompson's catalogues not only before, but also after his appointment to the Fitzwilliam Directorship. He believed that Thompson's manuscripts would come to his Museum, and was shocked when Thompson announced in December 1917 that he would sell his collection at auction. The bitter disappointment left Cockerell wiser and perhaps less confident that private collections he had built would come to the Fitzwilliam.

The largest private collection that Cockerell never worked on, but still hoped to tap into, was that of Thomas Phillipps who had hoarded over 60,000 volumes at Cheltenham. The manuscript that Cockerell coveted most was the set of thirteenth-century Old Testament leaves known as the Morgan Picture Bible from which he owned a leaf himself.[42] He tried to buy the leaves from Phillipps's grandson and heir, Thomas FitzRoy Fenwick, first for Yates Thompson in 1904 and then for Dyson Perrins in 1908, but failed both times. Later, he was hoping to acquire them for the Fitzwilliam, but Belle da Costa Greene secured them for Pierpont Morgan in 1916. This provoked a frosty exchange with the jealous Fitzwilliam Director. The ice would melt into a lifelong friendship in the 1920s, when Greene was Cockerell's guest in Cambridge and he her guest in New York. In 1927 he would publish the Old Testament leaves as J. P. Morgan's presentation volume for the Roxburghe Club.[43]

In 1904, Cockerell met Thomas Henry Riches and his first wife, Mary. The son of a wealthy mine owner from Cardiff, the aptly named Riches was a Cambridge *alumnus* and a successful Plymouth businessman. Cockerell was not impressed by Thomas and Mary's collections, but this changed in 1908 when the widowed Riches married Katherine Linnell. As the granddaughter of the painter John Linnell, William Blake's last great patron, Katherine had inherited a collection of Blake's works and was keen to expand it. The Director encouraged this while also steering the Riches towards illuminated manuscripts. The Riches were among the Fitzwilliam's most generous benefactors, bequeathing their entire collection as well as financing purchases ranging from Oriental ceramics and Private Press books to Japanese prints. They helped Cockerell create the Fitzwilliam's outstanding collection of William Blake's works, buying everything they wanted at the historic Linnell sale at Christie's in 1918.[44]

Cockerell was particularly adept at befriending the wives of his patrons. Jane Morris, Lady Georgiana Burne-Jones, Lady Anne Blunt, Katherine Riches and Edith Beatty are the best-known examples. Yates Thompson's wife was the only exception – Cockerell knew she did not like him and blamed her for his failure to secure Thompson's manuscripts for his Museum.

When Yates Thompson told Cockerell in December 1917 that he would sell his collection, Cockerell accused, pleaded and in the end agreed to buy one manuscript prior to the sale for £4000 – twice what he had negotiated for Yates Thompson's purchase of it from Ruskin's heir in 1901. The manuscript was Ruskin's favourite 'St Louis Psalter,' which, as Cockerell had established, was a combined Psalter-Hours made for Louis IX's sister, Isabelle of France, and the sister book of the Psalter made for St Louis himself.[45] It was Thomas Riches who lent Cockerell the princely sum of £4000 on short notice and interest-free, and contributed £250 to the fundraising campaign. The story has been told before[46] and needs no repeating here except to illustrate another of Cockerell's acquisition tactics. The Director had made a special point about involving only Cambridge men in his campaign for the Psalter-Hours, but two years later he was still short of £493. On 31 October 1919 he secured the sum over dinner with J. P. Morgan who had received an honorary degree earlier that day and thus qualified – only just – as a member of the university.[47] This opportunistic approach was the most desperate of Cockerell's stratagems.

Of the 11 manuscripts that came to the Museum with Thomas Riches' bequest in 1950, 10 had been acquired on Cockerell's advice.[48] Eight of them were purchased at the Yates Thompson's sales. Another was bought on Cockerell's instruction at the 1932 sale of Alfred Chester Beatty's manuscripts. This brings us to the last major figure whose collection Cockerell helped to build, but failed to secure for the Fitzwilliam.

Thomas Riches was not the only buyer bidding on Cockerell's advice at the Yates Thompson sales. Beatty was doing the same – he bought five of Thompson's manuscripts. An American engineer who had amassed a considerable fortune from his international mining business, Beatty was already buying manuscripts when Cockerell met him in 1916.[49] Unimpressed, the Fitzwilliam Director worked hard to bring Beatty's collection to an acceptable standard. He wasted no time in recruiting him as a Friend of the Fitzwilliam and praised his generosity in the annual *Bulletin of the Friends* for 1920 where Beatty's 'name again heads the list of subscribers.' In 1919 Beatty lent four of his finest Persian manuscripts to the Museum and in 1928 ceded one of them, a copy of Hafiz's *Diwan*, in a peculiar transaction orchestrated by Cockerell. In 1922 Wilfrid Blunt had bequeathed to the Fitzwilliam a copy of Ferdowsi's *Shahnama* that had belonged to William Morris together with £45 to be spent on another Oriental manuscript.[50] Although this sum was well below the market value of the *Diwan*, Beatty accepted it. Next, he let Cockerell keep the £45 as his subscription to the Friends. This was an acquisition that made the most of old and new patrons. Cockerell received Beatty's manuscript for free and transferred Blunt's sum to the Friends' fund.

Cockerell was planning to herd into the Fitzwilliam all of Beatty's manuscripts and much more. Beatty's wife, Edith, was buying Impressionists and, unlike Mrs Yates Thompson, was very fond of Cockerell. The Beattys' country house in Kent offered a much-needed retreat for the overworked Director, allowing him to complete publications. In October 1920 the Beattys invited Cockerell to join them for a trip to America. He toured the East coast, visiting libraries, museums and private collections in New York, Boston, Philadelphia and Washington where he was treated, in his own words, as 'the Emperor of Manuscripta.'[51] He was grateful for Belle da Costa Greene's hospitality at the Morgan Library, but could not resist offering advice. His diary records that he spent a day at the Morgan 'looking through the inferior books which are numerous and ought to be got rid of.'[52]

Belle Greene introduced Cockerell to Dr Rosenbach in whose stock the Fitzwilliam Director made one of his greatest discoveries. On 10 November 1920 he identified six Psalter leaves illuminated and signed by William de Brailes – the artist he had first encountered in the Hours he bought for Dyson Perrins in 1906. He persuaded Beatty to buy the leaves for $6,000.[53] In 1930 Cockerell would publish his discoveries on William de Brailes in a monograph presented to the Roxburghe Club by Beatty.[54] Two years later Beatty decided to sell his manuscripts.

As with the Yates Thompson sales, Cockerell focused on one item – the de Brailes leaves. He asked Beatty to reserve them until 6 June 1932; if he failed to raise the £3,500 needed, the leaves were to be sold at auction the following day. This story has been told too,[55] but it is worth mentioning briefly as an example of the Director's flexible approach in what was his last great fundraising campaign. At first, Cockerell adopted the same strategy that he had used for Isabelle's Psalter-Hours. He approached an old patron, Mrs Oppenheimer, but she was about to undergo surgery. He changed tactics and applied to a public grant giving body, the National Art Collections Fund (now the Art Fund). Established in 1903 to help British art institutions acquire works sold by private collectors, the Art Fund seemed the obvious solution at a time when many of Cockerell's benefactors were affected by the Depression.

As soon as Cockerell contacted the Art Fund, its Chairman, Sir Robert Witt, scheduled a meeting of the Committee for 18 May 1932. For two weeks Cockerell lobbied Committee members at receptions, dinners and at home.[56] Anticipating his success, he drafted announcements for the press before the final decision was made on 18 May. Cockerell was pleased and Beatty must have been even more so, especially after the sale on 7 June which realized a meagre £23,000 and was described in *The New York Times Book Review* as a 'dismal showing.' The campaign for the de Brailes leaves was a classic example, in Cockerell's own words, of 'the bullying and wire-pulling for which I am justly famous.'[57] His tactics, however, strained his relationship with some of the Committee members, especially the Chairman who felt out-manoeuvred. Despite his success, Cockerell never approached the Art Fund again.

Let us look at his last stratagem: luring collectors of other media into the buying of manuscripts. Our final examples constitute the cream of Lord Lee's collection which came to the Fitzwilliam in 1954.[58] Lord Lee of Fareham (1868–1947) is hardly thought of as a manuscript collector. He is best known as the personal military secretary of Lloyd George, the life-long friend of Theodore Roosevelt and the politician who gave Chequers to the British nation for the use of successive Prime Ministers. He is also remembered as the main force behind the foundation of the Courtauld Institute in 1932 and the transfer of the Warburg Institute from Hamburg to London in 1933 (which required clearance from M.I.5).[59]

Following a prominent military career in Canada in the 1890s, Lee married the daughter of a New York banker, returned to England and served as Conservative M.P. for Fareham in Hampshire. In 1922 he retired from politics and turned to art politics and collecting. Lee's passion was for Old Masters (his paintings are at the Courtauld Gallery in London) and metalwork (his silver is at the Royal Ontario Museum in Toronto). Ten of his illuminated manuscripts are also in Toronto, but another five are at the Fitzwilliam. How did this come to be?

After discussions with his friend, Vincent Massey, the Canadian High Commissioner in London who was about to become Chancellor of the University of Toronto, Lord Lee shipped his collection to Toronto in 1940 – officially as a gift to the University, but really for safe keeping during the war. In 1946 Lord Lee asked to have some of his treasures back. There are at least two reasons for this change of heart. First, throughout the 1930s he had been campaigning for keeping art in England and when he offered his collections to Toronto, he did so with the utmost secrecy, lest news reach the English art establishment. Second, the manuscripts (and probably the silver as well) may have been promised to the Fitzwilliam. In the 1960s, Sydney Cockerell and Kenneth Clark (who was Lord Lee's executor) believed that all of Lee's manuscripts were in Cambridge.[60]

It was Cockerell who lured Lord Lee into the world of manuscripts. In the 1920s he was showing Lee illuminations related to his paintings. He was also campaigning for Cambridge University to offer Lee an honorary degree – Cockerell's stratagem of creating a Cambridge connection for his benefactors. The doctorate was presented to Lord Lee on 5 June 1931. After the ceremony he and other recipients of honorary degrees joined the Vice Chancellor and Sydney Cockerell for a reception at the Fitzwilliam and a display of artworks, including silver and illuminated manuscripts. The reception was carefully timed – on 5 June Cockerell held the private view for his new extension, the Courtauld Galleries funded by the family of Lord Lee's friend, Samuel Courtauld. The following year, he secured Lord Lee's advocacy with the Art Fund in support for the purchase of the de Brailes leaves.

Two of Lord Lee's manuscripts now at the Fitzwilliam – a thirteenth-century English Psalter and a fifteenth-century Flemish Psalter-Hours – were sent back from Toronto and presented to the Fitzwilliam in 1954 by Lady Lee in accordance with her late husband's wishes.[61] The other three volumes now in Cambridge had been bought after the dispatch of Lee's collection to Toronto in 1940 and must have been reserved for the Fitzwilliam.

In June 1946, Lee paid Quaritch £750 for a fifteenth-century Missal by the Sienese painter-illuminator Sano di Pietro – a manuscript in tune with Lee's interest in Italian painting.[62] In 1943 Lee bought the c. 1470 copy of Suetonius' *Lives of the Caesars* for £125 from Davis and Orioli, the antiquarian booksellers in Wallingford, Berkshire.[63] As a Humanistic manuscript, it is a stranger in Lee's collection. Perhaps he bought it at the instigation of Sydney Cockerell, the first champion of Humanistic manuscripts in England.[64]

The final manuscript confirms Cockerell's involvement in Lee's collecting. It is the *Grandes Heures* commissioned by Philip the Bold, Duke of Burgundy, in Paris in the 1370s and completed for his grandson, Philip the Good c. 1450.[65] It came into Lord Lee's possession in June 1940, just as the rest of his manuscripts were being shipped to Toronto. In November 1939, Cockerell had discovered the manuscript in the possession of the wife of the rector of Symondsbury, Dorset, only a few miles from the Rectory at Bridport where Lee had been born almost exactly 70 years before Cockerell's visit. Cockerell liked coincidences as much as he liked manuscripts and friendships. All three of Lee's final acquisitions were made after Cockerell's retirement, but he must have advocated for their purchase with the familiar argument that they could find a permanent home in the Fitzwilliam. Lord Lee obliged, like many others.

Rubbing shoulders with prominent collectors, Cockerell could not resist the temptation to join their ranks. The encounter with Ruskin and Morris made him upgrade from his teenage shells, fossils, butterflies, stamps and coins to autograph letters, drawings, fine printing and – his true passion – illuminated manuscripts. While he could hardly match the purchasing power of Yates Thompson, Dyson Perrins or Alfred Chester Beatty, his expertise and shrewd negotiation skills allowed him to acquire manuscripts well beyond the means of a free-lance cataloguer or an underpaid Museum Director.[66] A remarkable achievement for a scholar and a father of three who was also looking after a seriously ill wife in the age before the NHS, his collection was a real tribute to his profound knowledge of manuscripts and the salerooms.

Faithful to the lessons of Ruskin and Morris, Cockerell had a preference for French and English Gothic illumination. Under Blunt's influence, he acquired Koran fragments and Persian manuscripts. He also developed a passion for Italian Humanistic texts and, to his surprise, for Flemish illumination. Three of the manuscripts sold at Dyson Perrins's sales in 1958–1959 were presented to the Fitzwilliam by Henry Davis in 1975. Among them was one of the first manuscripts to arouse Cockerell's interest in Flemish illumination: the Hours that he bought for Dyson Perrins in 1906 and brought to Cambridge to examine alongside other Flemish manuscripts in 1907, while lobbying for the Fitzwilliam Directorship.[67]

It seems surprising that Cockerell worked so hard to persuade others to leave their manuscripts to the Fitzwilliam, but did not leave his own. There are several reasons. First, his family duties: though hardly destitute, he was not a rich man and when he sold his collection in the 1950s, he distributed the profits among his children. Second, Cockerell never felt that Cambridge University acknowledged his contribution by supporting his Museum or paying him a decent salary. Third, he was never to be associated with anything less than first-class material. Fond and proud as he was of his collection, Cockerell knew that it would not stand up to the treasures already at the Fitzwilliam, including those acquired during his Directorship, which is still considered the most dynamic, enriching and transformative period in the Museum's 200-year history.

Notes

1 London, British Library, Add. MS 52645.

2 Stella Panayotova, *I Turned It into a Palace: Sydney Cockerell and the Fitzwilliam Museum* (Cambridge: Fitzwilliam Museum, 2008), pp. 198–201; William Stoneman, '"Variously Employed": The Pre-Fitzwilliam Career of Sydney Carlyle Cockerell,' in *Art, Academia and the Trade: Sir Sydney Cockerell (1867–1962)*, ed. by Stella Panayotova (Cambridge: Cambridge Bibliographical Society, 2010), pp. 345–62; Shane Carmody, '"Vain, Aggressive and Somewhat Quarrelsome": The Enduring Impact of Sir Sydney Cockerell on the Melbourne Collections,' in Panayotova, *Art*, pp. 421–455.

3 Wilfrid Blunt, *Cockerell: Sydney Carlyle Cockerell, Friend of Ruskin and William Morris and Director of the Fitzwilliam Museum, Cambridge* (London: H. Hamilton, 1964); Panayotova, *Palace*, pp. 6–51.

4 Christopher de Hamel, 'Cockerell as Entrepreneur,' *The Book Collector*, 55.1 (2006), 49–72; Richard A. Linenthal, 'Sydney Cockerell: Bookseller in All but Name,' in Panayotova, *Art*, pp. 363–386.

5 Christopher de Hamel, 'Cockerell as Museum Director,' *The Book Collector*, 55.2 (2006), 201–223; Panayotova, *Palace*, pp. 52–213; Stella Panayotova, 'St Cockerellius: The Director-Collector,' in Panayotova, *Art*, pp. 387–420; Lucilla Burn, *The Fitzwilliam Museum: A History* (London: Philip Wilson, 2016), pp. 116–144.
6 Cockerell's diary entry for 30 April 1932. London, British Library, Add. MS 52670.
7 Panayotova, *Palace*, pp. 60–63; Burn, *History*, pp. 124–125.
8 Panayotova, *Palace*, pp. 186–205.
9 Panayotova, *Palace*, pp. 66–70.
10 Cockerell's 1913 and 1924 annual reports to the University of Cambridge.
11 Panayotova, *Palace*, pp. 193–195.
12 Panayotova, 'St Cockerellius,' p. 404.
13 Panayotova, *Palace*, pp. 15–16, 29, 201–202.
14 Blunt, *Cockerell*, p. 135.
15 Panayotova, *Palace*, p. 201; Carmody, 'Vain,' pp. 428–447.
16 Martin Hardie to Cockerell, 6 June 1931: *The Best of Friends: Further Letters to Sydney Carlyle Cockerell*, ed. by Viola Meynell (London: Rupert Hart-Davis, 1956), p. 42.
17 Cockerell's diary entry for 29 May 1932: London, British Library, Add. MS 52670.
18 The words of a Fellow of Jesus College were quoted in Cockerell's obituary in the Jesus College Cambridge Society Annual Report for 1962, which described him as 'a persistent and most successful beggar on behalf of the Fitzwilliam.'
19 Blunt, *Cockerell*, p. 142.
20 Sydney Cockerell to Louis Clarke, 23 December 1943: Fitzwilliam Museum, MS 1577–1977.
21 We cannot do justice here to Cockerell's acquisitions across all media and they have been dealt with elsewhere: Panayotova, *Palace*, pp. 83–185; Panayotova, 'St Cockerellius.'
22 Christopher de Hamel, 'Introduction: Sydney Cockerell and Medieval Manuscripts in the Twentieth Century,' in Panayotova, *Art*, pp. 339–343.
23 Sotheby's, London, 5 June 1908 (Hodgson's sale), lot 625, which is now Fitzwilliam Museum, MS 269.
24 Copies of Cockerell's letters to Charles and Richard Davis of 147 New Bond Street dated 13 February, 18 February and 10 March 1909 in the Museum's Letter Book: Fitzwilliam Museum Archive, 9.
25 Panayotova, *Palace*, pp. 73–81; Panayotova, 'St Cockerellius,' pp. 390–395; Burn, *History*, pp. 126–128.
26 Fitzwilliam Museum, MS 294. See www.fitzmuseum.cam.ac.uk/illuminated/; Nigel Morgan and Stella Panayotova, *A Catalogue of Western Book Illumination in the Fitzwilliam Museum and the Cambridge Colleges*, Part I, vol. 2, 2 vols. (London and Turnhout: Harvey Miller and Brepols, 2009), no. 245; and the entries in *Colour: The Art and Science of Illuminated Manuscripts*, ed. by Stella Panayotova (London and Turnhout: Harvey Miller and Brepols, 2016), nos. 89, 105.
27 Panayotova, *Palace*, pp. 73–76; Panayotova, 'St Cockerellius,' pp. 392–393.
28 Cockerell's diary entry for 7 November 1899: London, British Library, Add. MS 52636.
29 John Ruskin, *The Diaries of John Ruskin*, ed. by Joan Evans and John Howard Whitehouse, vol. 2, 3 vols. (Oxford: Oxford University Press, 1956–1959) (1958), p. 491.

30 Ruskin's letters to Norton dated 25 February and 2 June 1861 are at Harvard University, the Houghton Library, bMS Am 1088 (5913) and (5914); John Ruskin and Charles Eliot Norton, *The Correspondence of John Ruskin and Charles Eliot Norton*, ed. by John Lewis Bradley and Ian Ousby (Cambridge: Cambridge University Press, 1987), pp. 60–65.

31 Fitzwilliam Museum, MS 242; Panayotova, *Palace*, pp. 8–9. For digital images, with description and technical analyses, see www.fitzmuseum.cam.ac.uk/illuminated/

32 Fitzwilliam Museum, MSS 116–1978 to 127–1978; William Morris, *The Collected Letters of William Morris*, ed. by Norman Kelvin, vol. 4, 4 vols. (Princeton: Princeton University Press, 1984–1996), (1996), nos. 2278–2341.

33 Blunt, *Cockerell*, pp. 67–76, 108–114, 175–191; Panayotova, *Palace*, pp. 28–33.

34 Charles Fairfax Murray bought a small selection, while the bulk of Morris's library went to the Manchester manufacturer Richard Bennett.

35 Blunt, *Cockerell*, p. 137.

36 Panayotova, *Palace*, pp. 40–43.

37 *Ibid.*, pp. 160–163.

38 Cockerell's diary entry for 6 July 1909: London, British Library, Add. MS 52646.

39 Lord Crewe to Cockerell, 26 June 1933: Cambridge University Library, Cambridge University Registry 30.4, item 631; Panayotova, *Palace*, p. 172, figs. 2.124–2.125.

40 Christopher de Hamel, 'Entrepreneur,' pp. 65–67.

41 For 'the de Brailes Hours' (London, British Library, Add. MS 49999), see www.bl.uk/catalogues/illuminatedmanuscripts/record.asp?MSID=6430

42 For the Bible (New York, Morgan Library & Museum, MS M.638) see http://corsair.themorgan.org/cgi-bin/Pwebrecon.cgi?BBID=158530. For Cockerell's leaf (Los Angeles, J. Paul Getty Museum, MS Ludwig I 6), see www.getty.edu/art/col lection/objects/1342/unknown-maker-leaf-from-the-morgan-picture-bible-french-1250/. See also the essay by Toby Burrows in this volume.

43 Sydney C. Cockerell, Montague R. James and Charles J. Ffoulkes, *A Book of Old Testament Illustrations of the Middle of the Thirteenth Century* (Cambridge: Cambridge University Press for the Roxburghe Club, 1927).

44 Panayotova, 'St Cockerellius,' pp. 397–400.

45 Sydney C. Cockerell, *A Psalter and Hours Executed before 1270 for a Lady Connected with St. Louis* (London: Chiswick Press, 1905). For the Psalter-Hours of Isabelle of France (Fitzwilliam Museum, MS 300), see www.fitzmuseum.cam.ac.uk/illuminated/ and the entry in Panayotova, *Colour*, no. 61. For the Psalter of Saint Louis (Paris, Bibliothèque nationale de France, MS lat. 10525), see http://archivesetmanuscrits.bnf.fr/ark:/12148/cc78039r; for a full digital copy, see http://gallica.bnf.fr/ark:/12148/btv1b8447877n

46 Blunt, *Cockerell*, pp. 144–148; Stella Panayotova, 'A Ruskinian Project with a Cockerellian Flavour,' *The Book Collector*, 54.3 (2005), 357–374; Christopher de Hamel, 'Cockerell as Collector,' *The Book Collector*, 55.3 (2006), 339–366; Panayotova, *Palace*, pp. 149–155.

47 Blunt, *Cockerell*, p. 202.

48 Panayotova, *Palace*, p. 156; Stella Panayotova, 'Cockerell and Riches,' in *The Medieval Book: Glosses from Friends and Colleagues of Christopher de Hamel*, ed. by James H. Marrow, Richard Linenthal and William Noel ('t Goy-Houten: Hes and De Graaf, 2010), pp. 377–386.

49 Christopher de Hamel, 'Director,' pp. 214–217; Laura Cleaver, 'The Western Manuscript Collection of Alfred Chester Beatty (ca. 1915–1930),' *Manuscript Studies*, 2.2 (2017), 445–482. See also the essay by Laura Cleaver and Danielle Magnusson in this volume.
50 The two manuscripts are Fitzwilliam Museum, MS 311 (*Shahnama*) and MS 323 (*Diwan*); Panayotova, *Palace*, pp. 29, 156.
51 Blunt, *Cockerell*, p. 253.
52 Cockerell's diary entries for October-November 1920: London, British Library, Add. MS 52657.
53 Cockerell's diary entries for 10–11 November 1920: London, British Library, Add. MS 52657.
54 Sydney C. Cockerell, *The Work of W. de Brailes, an English Illuminator of the Thirteenth Century* (Cambridge: Cambridge University Press for the Roxburghe Club, 1930).
55 Christopher de Hamel, 'Director,' pp. 216–217; Panayotova, *Palace*, pp. 157–158; Panayotova, 'St Cockerellius,' pp. 401–403.
56 Cockerell's diary entry for 29 April 1932 reads: 'I went first to Hertford House to see David Meldrum about the Nat. Art Collections Fund's buying the 6 Brailes leaves – he was very sympathetic. Then to Alec Martin at Christie's for the same purpose. He said he would give his full support. Then to Sotheby's and got des Graz to endorse his letter with the statement that my option lasts until 6 June.' [Then to a Royal Academy private view where he met many friends.] 'Talked about the Brailes leaves to Lord Lee of Fareham, Sir William Llewellyn and Charles Aitken, all on the Committee of the N.A.C. fund and got their support. Talked about them also to Lord Crawford and Lord Conway … Home very tired by the 7.10.' London, British Library, Add. MS 52670.
57 Blunt, *Cockerell*, p. 144.
58 Stella Panayotova, 'From Toronto to Cambridge: The Illuminated Manuscripts of Lord Lee of Fareham,' *University of Toronto Quarterly*, 77.2 (2008), 673–710; repr. in *Transactions of the Cambridge Bibliographical Society*, 13.2 (2005, published in 2008), 187–220.
59 The telegram sent by M.I.5 to Lord Lee survives in the General Correspondence for 1933–1942 in the Warburg Institute Archives.
60 The files on one of Lord Lee's manuscripts in Toronto preserve a letter sent in 1961 by Eleanor Spencer, Professor of Fine Arts in Baltimore, to Mr Brett at the Royal Ontario Museum: 'I wrote enthusiastically about the De Giac Hours to Sir Sydney Cockerell, who replied that Lord Lee's manuscripts were all in the Fitzwilliam Museum, that Sir Kenneth Clark had confirmed this fact. Please, set me straight.'
61 Fitzwilliam Museum, MS 2–1954 and MS 4–1954. For MS 2–1954, see Francis Wormald and Phyllis M. Giles, *A Descriptive Catalogue of the Additional Illuminated Manuscripts in the Fitzwilliam Museum* (Cambridge: Cambridge University Press, 1982), pp. 475–479. For MS 4–1954, see Morgan and Panayotova, *Catalogue*, vol. 2, no. 167.
62 Fitzwilliam Museum, MS 6–1954. Nigel Morgan, Stella Panayotova and Suzanne Reynolds, *A Catalogue of Western Book Illumination in the Fitzwilliam Museum and the Cambridge Colleges*, Part II, vol. 2, 2 vols. (London and Turnhout: Harvey Miller and Brepols, 2011), no. 235; and the entry in Panayotova, *Colour*, no. 7.

63 Fitzwilliam Museum, MS 5–1954. Morgan, Panayotova and Reynolds, *Catalogue*, vol. 2, no. 293.

64 Christopher de Hamel, 'Director,' p. 218; Christopher de Hamel, 'Collector,' p. 344.

65 Fitzwilliam Museum, MS 3–1954. See www.fitzmuseum.cam.ac.uk/illuminated/; Morgan and Panayotova, *Catalogue*, vol. 2, no. 175; and the entry in Panayotova, *Colour*, no. 29.

66 Christopher de Hamel, 'Medieval and Renaissance Manuscripts from the Library of Sir Sydney Cockerell (1867–1962),' *The British Library Journal*, 13 (1987), 186–210; see also Christopher de Hamel, 'Collector'; Panayotova, *Palace*, pp. 36–38.

67 Fitzwilliam Museum, MS 1058–1975. See www.fitzmuseum.cam.ac.uk/illuminated/; Morgan and Panayotova, *Catalogue*, vol. 2, no. 230; and the entry in Panayotova, *Colour*, no. 108.

7 Spending a fortune

Robert Edward Hart, bibliophile and numismatist, an industrialist collector in Blackburn, Lancashire

Cynthia Johnston

If Liverpool and Manchester served as the great metropolises of commerce during the Industrial Revolution, the small towns of Pennine Lancashire were the places of 'making.' Blackburn was one of the most successful of these communities, competing against the towns of Bury, Rochdale, Bolton and Oldham in terms of the production of cotton cloth. As well as the cotton mills themselves, associated industries, such as the production of tallow and oils, as well as the manufacture of driving ropes, profited handsomely from the industrial revolution.[1] Driving ropes were an essential component of the cotton mills, turning the shafts that delivered power to the looms. The invention of the 'Lambeth Power Rope' by Thomas Hart, R. E. Hart's father, transformed their business, Thomas Hart Rope Works, from a comfortable family concern to a multi-national company that produced immense profits.[2] Robert Edward Hart was the eldest son of the fourth generation of this family (see Figure 7.1). The span of his life from 1878 to 1946 coincided with the apex and decline of the fortunes of the industrialists of the northwest. Hart's ability to spend was matched by his inclination to do so, most particularly on his collector's passion for rare books and coins.

This chapter will focus on Hart's collection of books and coins which were bequeathed to the Blackburn Public Library upon his death. I will argue that Hart's gift to the town was unusual in its bibliographical significance, but it was also part of a philanthropic movement which was particularly pronounced in these regional centres. The competition between the regional centres of cotton production, with their breathtaking expansion from quiet market towns to teeming mini-metropolises in the space of a generation, was certainly a key factor in the donation of spectacular personal collections to local museums or libraries. The enactment of Christian values such as community welfare, self-improvement and good works were, I argue, a key motivational factor in both the accumulation and the eventual bequest of these industrialist collections, not to the nation, but, as Hart put it, to the people 'of my native town.'[3] In *The People's Galleries*, Giles

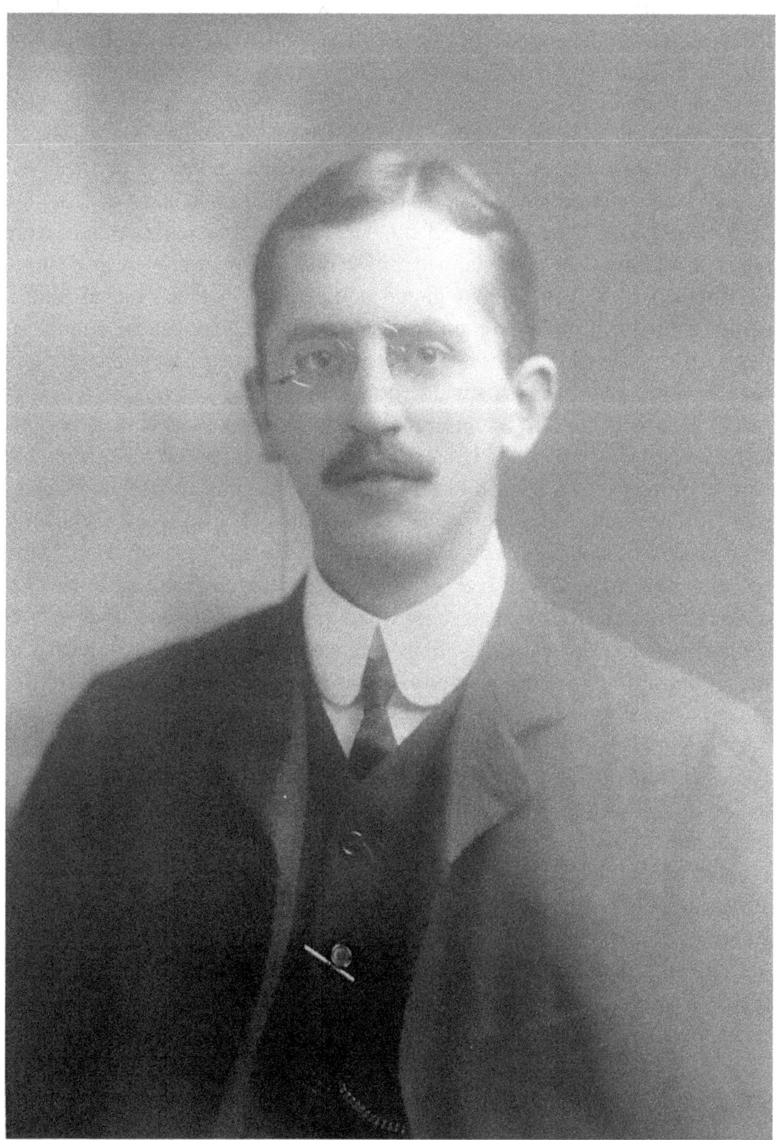

Figure 7.1 Robert Edward Hart as a young man, c. 1897–1899

(Reproduced with the permission of the Blackburn Museum and Art Gallery)

Waterfield argued that the agenda of the new public museums – founded in the metropolitan industrial centres of Manchester, Leeds, Liverpool, Glasgow and Nottingham during the late nineteenth and early twentieth centuries – was to engage with a new audience, the urban working class.[4] Waterfield perceived these as a new type of museum, a municipal gallery, with a decidedly liberal agenda. The new museums found their audiences and enjoyed tremendous contemporary success. There is no doubt that some of the same civic forces were at work in the Pennine production towns, but there were other local impulses that defined the central motivations of collectors. Paternalism, civic pride and regional competition, perhaps mixed with a certain amount of guilt, prompted those who lived amongst the communities which laboured in their industries to give back what gave them pleasure for the betterment of those specific communities.

The Hart collection of manuscripts, rare books and coins is certainly one of the most important in the United Kingdom with regard to the quality and variety of its contents. Hart himself considered his coins to be the more significant collection, with his complete run of Roman Imperial coins which we now know is equaled only by that held by the British Museum. Hart's coin collection includes 1,250 Greek Imperial coins, 1,865 Roman coins, 70 Byzantine coins and 2,125 British coins which range from late medieval to Victorian examples.[5] Hart seems to have inaugurated his coin collecting early in life. A daguerreotype photograph in the Hart archives of a twentieth birthday present consisting of a tray of collectible eighteenth- and nineteenth-century coins seems to indicate an early passion (see Figure 7.2).

Hart's book collection contains over 800 items, with 500 rare books, including 21 medieval manuscripts, 50 incunabula with representatives of most of the major locations for early print production in Europe, Islamic manuscripts of the eighteenth and nineteenth centuries, cuneiform tablets, Torah scrolls as well as important editions of books from nineteenth- and twentieth-century private presses including William Morris's Kelmscott Press. The question that I will address here is what motivated Hart to collect and to give? What is the dynamic between the collector and the intended public recipient?

Social historical context

The intensely populated town inhabited by Robert Edward Hart was a world away from the environs of the Blackburn of his grandparents' day. As Derek Beattie points out, the population of Blackburn in 1880 was over 100,000, and, 100 years previously, it had been just 5,000.[6] In the *Diary and Buyers' Guide of 1897* printed by Henry Bannerman and Sons, a Manchester based firm that invested in spinning and manufacturing cotton cloth,

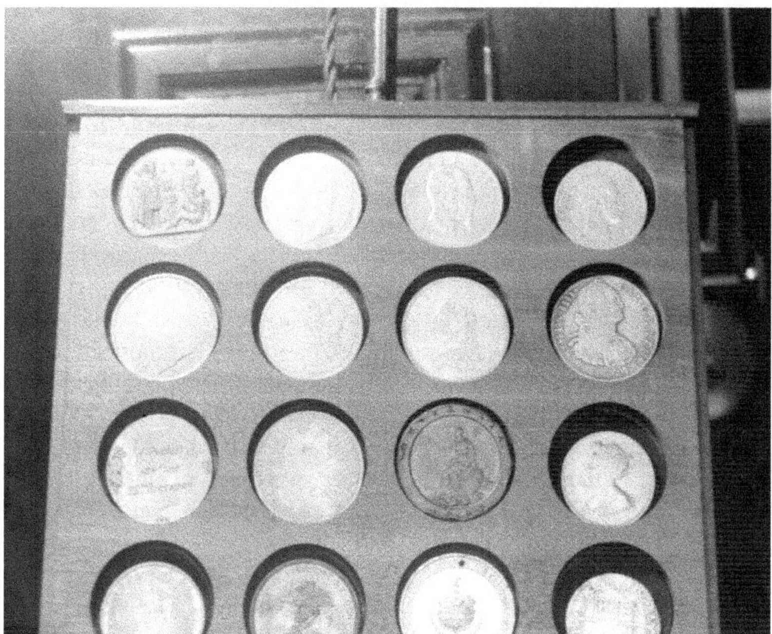

Figure 7.2 A tray of collectible coins; second from bottom left is marked 'Present for the 20th Birthday'

(Reproduced with the permission of the Blackburn Museum and Art Gallery)

Blackburn is described as one of the most important manufacturing districts in Lancashire.[7]

> As the writer approaches the town via steam tram, he notes that the town spreads out before us, dim from the smoke of many chimneys, and with a labyrinth of streets filled with monotonous-featured habitations: Blackburn in this aspect, however, differing not greatly in somberness from many other industrial towns in the county. When we have reached an open space in the centre of town we find the parish church, the railway station, and many buildings architecturally pleasant to look upon, we have evidences of the modern spirit manifesting itself here as elsewhere, the earnest of brighter things to be.[8]

Amongst these buildings were the Public Free Library, the museum, public baths and a 'beautifully picturesque public park' (Corporation Park).[9] There was also a new Technical College, now part of Blackburn University Centre.[10] The crucial information delivered by the *Buyers' Guide* was that, in 1897, there was a population of 120,000 inhabitants in the town, 1,200,000 spindles were in use and the town's 75,000 looms produced miles of cotton cloth every day.[11] The readers of the *Buyers' Guide* were in a fertile land of commercial opportunity.

An important factor in Blackburn's social structure was the absence of an overarching aristocratic class.[12] From the 1820s, Blackburn's political structure was dominated by middle-class families, albeit middle-class families who were accumulating vast fortunes, but who had come from undistinguished backgrounds. Many had arrived in Blackburn during the first decades of the nineteenth century attracted by the opportunities for commerce in the manufacture of cotton. Beattie argues that a 'middle class elite … controlled Blackburn from c. 1850 to 1914.'[13] The most successful of the early cotton entrepreneurs who had arrived in Blackburn in the last decades of the eighteenth century invested in the factory system.[14] Those who had made their fortunes first, and best, rose to become the social elite of the town. Some of the most financially successful families sold their mills and moved elsewhere, sometimes investing in land, and establishing themselves as a new landed gentry. Anthony Howe notes that some of the 'cotton masters,' the newly wealthy social class that emerged from the industrial revolution, such as the Peels and the Arkwrights, aspired to and successfully joined the landed gentry.[15] However, Beattie observes that the sales of these valuable mills were made to local businessmen, not to outsiders.[16] The buyers were men with middle-class backgrounds who controlled not only the financial but also the political power in the town. Instead of migrating away from the mills that were their source of wealth, the mill owners and those whose industries were associated with the cotton trade often remained resident and closely connected with the running not only of their businesses but of their communities themselves. Instead of disassociating themselves from the source of their wealth, as Howe observes, the cotton masters develop a 'self-sufficient bourgeoisie lifestyle, based on occupation, intermarriage, parliamentary and municipal control … [of their local areas] and a certain measure of cultural and social dominance.'[17]

Although they may have sent their sons to elite public schools such as Eton, Harrow or Rugby, and then on to Cambridge or Oxford, these sons often returned to Blackburn to continue the family trade. These men established themselves in the suburban villas of West Park Road, an area that sits above the centre of the town. The houses were large and commodious, but they were not built to accommodate large numbers of staff or visitors. They were comfortable as opposed to ostentatious. The records of a Blackburn social club called the 'Union Club' indicate that its inaugural members included 'a good cross-section of the upper middle class drawn from the professional and commercial life of the town.'[18] The 32 members included attorneys, brewers, a corn miller, cotton mill owners, a Roman Catholic priest, a curate of the parish church, the superintendent of the police and a linen and cotton draper.[19] The compiler of the Union Club's centennial publication noted that 'To-day, in 1950, the tone of the membership seems to have suffered little change, in that the present-day members of the Club are of the same type and caliber as those who founded it a hundred years ago.'[20] Robert Edward Hart is elected a member in 1917, the year that the death of his father is noted in the minutes.[21] Edward Hart was a product and a member of this distinct social class, identified by Howe as 'the first distinctive industrial elite in British society.'[22]

Biography

The Harts' Spring Mill Rope Walk was established in 1797, and traded until the 1930s. In addition to this site, Thomas Hart, Edward's father, established the Lambeth Street Rope Walk in 1866. In 1928, this business was incorporated as Thomas Hart Ltd. There were other rope-making concerns in Blackburn. In *Industrial Heritage, a Guide to the Industrial Archaeology of Blackburn* published by the Hyndburn Local History Society, Mike Rothwell lists three other roperies: Simmons Street Rope walk, Hollin Bank Ropery and Mill Hill Rope Works.[23] The Harts' business predates all of these in its foundation, but all four roperies met the same fate, with Simmons ceasing business in 1930, and Thomas Hart Ltd. and Mill Hill both closing down in 1967. Hollin Bank continued to trade until 1974.[24] Always known as Edward, Robert Edward Hart was the eldest son of Thomas and Hannah Hart. Thomas Hart followed the pattern of both his father and his grandfather before him with regard to participating actively in the civic life of the town by serving as a member of quasi-political institutions.[25] Thomas Hart was treasurer of the Blackburn Guardian Society for the Protection of Trade for 45 years, and director of the Blackburn Chamber of Commerce for the same length of time. Both Thomas and Edward served as directors of the Blackburn Savings Bank. Thomas also served as a J.P., as had his father. Thomas Hart also gave his support and active participation to religious societies including the Society for Promoting Christianity among the Jews, the British and Foreign Bible Society, the Missionary Society and the Church Pastoral Aid Society. Edward Hart represented the Blackburn Chamber of Commerce during 1922–1923. He followed his father as treasurer for the Church Missions to the Jews and Blackburn Guardian Societies, and he became treasurer for the Blackburn Orphanage in 1908, a position he held until his death (see Figure 7.3). Thomas Hart was a founding member of the orphanage, the idea of James Dixon, a local journeyman joiner.[26] Peggy Cook, who recorded her recollections of her life as the

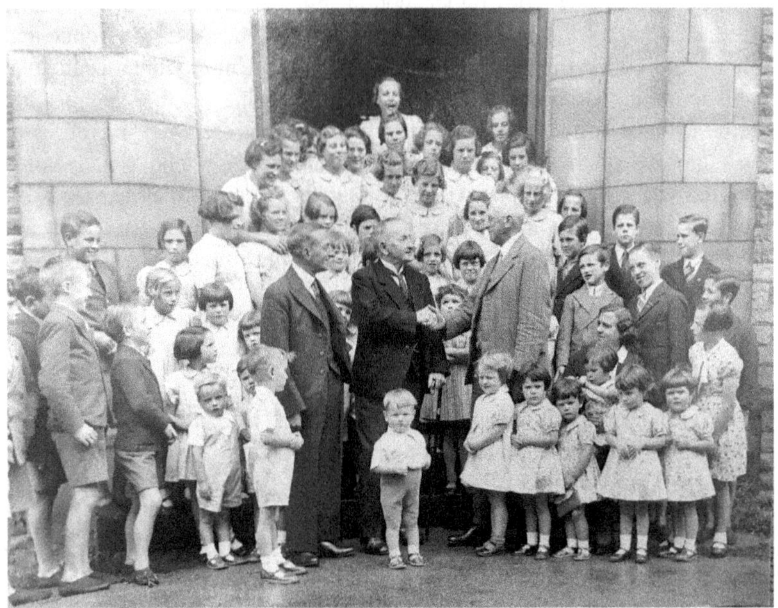

Figure 7.3 R. E. Hart, centre right, on the fiftieth anniversary of the Blackburn Orphanage

(Reproduced with the permission of the Blackburn Museum and Art Gallery)

Harts' parlour maid for 12 years, noted that Edward Hart visited the orphanage every Christmas morning before his own Christmas celebrations began.

As a child, Edward Hart was sent away from Blackburn to attend Horace Hill Preparatory School in Berkshire. The school reports from Hart's time at Horace Hill survive.[27] They show him struggling to catch up with his classmates in classical languages as well as French, but he eventually excelled in mathematics. Edward Hart attended Rugby School and Pembroke College, Cambridge where he read the Mechanical Science Tripos. This was a new degree established in 1893, just five years before Edward Hart began his Cambridge career.[28] The university was seemingly uncomfortable with using the term 'engineering' to describe its new tripos, and it was not until 1973 that Edward Hart's course was renamed as the Engineering Tripos.[29]

Hart's educational trajectory was not unusual in the context of his contemporaries, those whose fathers owned the core industrial concerns in Blackburn. Thomas Boys Lewis, who was slightly older than Hart (1869–1942), was born into a family of Blackburn cotton manufacturers and educated at Eton and King's College, Cambridge, where he read Classics. Lewis spent much of his professional life managing the family's Springfield Cotton

Spinning Mill. Lewis also donated his collections of Japanese prints from the eighteenth and nineteenth centuries, as well as his collection of religious icons, to the Blackburn Museum and Art Gallery. At the time of his bequest, the Japanese print collection was the largest of its type in Britain. Lewis's collection of religious icons is still the largest held by a museum in the U.K. In 1938, Lewis opened the Lewis Textile Museum in Blackburn, which contained examples of the machinery that propelled the textile industry. Lewis wished to document the physical evidence of an industry that he had watched arc and decline over the course of his life. The contents of the Lewis Textile Museum, closed in 2006, are now held by the Blackburn Museum and Art Gallery. Examples of looms, and their progressive technological development, are displayed in a dedicated gallery.

While Howe's cotton masters were able to afford the finest education for their sons, those sons must have experienced the restrictions of the rigid Edwardian class system in the context of their elite public schools and universities. Although no correspondence between Edward Hart and his university contemporaries survives, he must have been acutely aware of the difference between his own background and those of many of his collegiate cohort. However, he must also have already known others from his own background and geographical origin at Cambridge.

Hart left no written record of his experiences at Cambridge, but his affection for the university and for his college, Pembroke, is clear from the gifts he left to both. To his own college, Hart left a first edition copy of Edmund Spenser's *Faerie Queene*, along with a gift of £10,000, to be spent at the College's discretion.[30] To the University Library, he left a gift which transformed the Library's collections of early printed books.[31] These books were amongst Hart's most expensive acquisitions from Maggs Bros. booksellers in London. Maurice Ettinghausen's description of that transaction reveals much about Hart's approach as a collector:

> Some five or six years before the Second World War, by an extraordinary combination of circumstances, I was able to compile a special catalogue, of which only a few copies were issued, containing no less than five complete block books. My idea was to sell the set as a whole. What was my surprise, one morning, therefore, to greet an old customer, Mr R. E. Hart, who had been in the habit of buying moderately priced but interesting old books containing woodcut illustrations, armed with a proposition to buy the collection as a whole at a slightly reduced figure. He was carrying a small leather bag, as businessmen were wont to do in those Edwardian days. Our customer's proposition was accepted, and he thereupon produced no less than £25,000 in one-pound notes, which occupied two cashiers sometime in counting. He

> explained the reason for this method of payment: he did not want his bankers to know that he was spending so much money on books.[32]

The block books Hart bought that morning were printed in Germany in 1470: an *ars moriendi*, two *Biblia pauperum*, an *ars memoranda* and an Apocalypse. The sixth book included in Hart's 1946 bequest to the University Library was William Caxton's 1497 edition of Le Fevre's *History of Jason*. To Cambridge's Fitzwilliam Museum he left his collection of books of French eighteenth-century engravings. All three bequests were carefully curated to answer specific needs of the respective institutions. After Edward Hart's return to Blackburn following his university education, his achievement there, where he gained a 2.2 in the Mechanical Sciences Tripos, was a mark of distinction. He is often recorded as R. E. Hart, M.A., and indeed this distinction is noted by Peggy Morris in her account, and appears on his headstone in the churchyard of St Peter's church in the quiet village of Salesbury, beyond Blackburn.

A collection of Edwardian daguerreotype photographs held by the museum, most probably taken by Clifford Hart, the third child and second son of Thomas and Hannah Hart, show many family excursions and holidays, with a house on Grasmere called The Leas providing the setting for walks and picnics (see Figure 7.4). There are many photographs

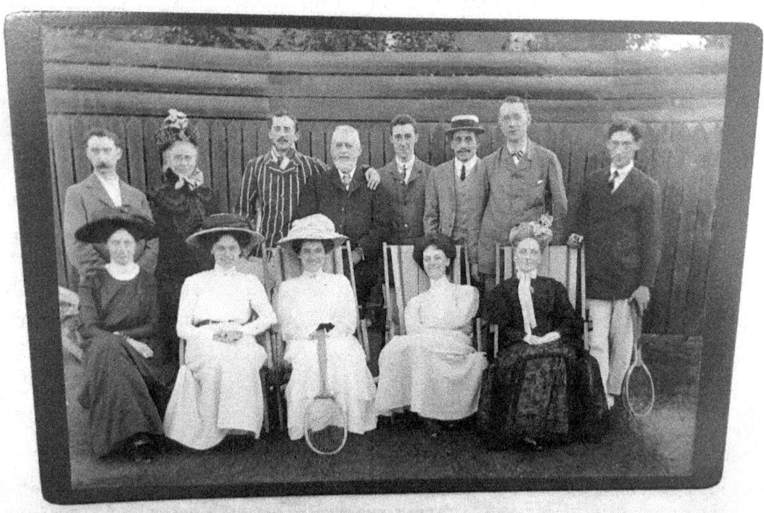

Figure 7.4 R. E. Hart, third from left back row, stands with his arm around his father Thomas, at a family tennis party, c. 1900

(Reproduced with the permission of the Blackburn Museum and Art Gallery)

of the family as a group, and also of the adolescent children, both male and female, playing cricket and tennis, demonstrating their shooting prowess and travelling by boat, steam tram and horse-drawn cart.

After his return from Cambridge, Edward Hart travelled to Canada as a representative of the Blackburn Chamber of Commerce, and there is evidence that he also travelled to Europe, through a surviving profile portrait created in Milan in 1906 in the Museum's archives (see Figure 7.5).

Collecting life

With regard to the genesis of Edward Hart's life as a collector, he must have been aware of the influence of Ruskin and certainly the Great Exhibition of 1851, but Hart himself does not record his first purchases, or whether they were of coins or books. The Victorian compulsion to order and categorize the world would have been observable to Edward Hart in the activities of others in his social class. The collections of Thomas Boys Lewis have already been mentioned, but the Hart family's friends, the Bowdler family, also mill owners who appear in the family photographs with the Harts on holiday at Grasmere, also collected. Arthur C. Bowdler (1842–1918), whose family had produced the Bowdler 'Family Shakespeare,' was a contemporary of Thomas Hart, and earnestly assembled a collection of coleoptera, with specimens gathered by Bowdler himself, as well as dried beetles sent to him by friends during their international travels. Clifford Hart sent specimens of beetles to Bowdler from South Africa and Dominica. Bowdler gave this collection of over 4,200 specimens of beetles from all over the globe, contained in 26 bespoke display boxes, to the Blackburn Museum in 1914 and it is certain that the Harts would have admired it while Bowdler was assembling his collection during their childhood. Indeed, it is possible, even probable, that Edward Hart began to collect as a boy. In *Goodbye to All That*, Robert Graves (1895–1985) notes that what distinguished him from his contemporaries at prep school, where he 'grew quarrelsome, boastful and domineering' was the fact that he 'collected coins instead of stamps.'[33] Graves reasoned that 'the value of coins seemed less fictitious to me.'[34] Hart may not have originally thought of collecting for any other purpose than his own pleasure, but a shift in attitude and intention made itself clear towards the end of Hart's life. The Blackburn Town Clerk, Mr Hindle, records that, on 12 July 1944, just over two years before Hart's death on 21 September 1946, Mr Hart had called in to see him.[35] Hart made it clear that he would like to make a gift to the town of his collections, and also to give the town the funds for an extension to the Public Library for the display of these collections.[36] He would like to induce the Corporation to shorten the length of time after the

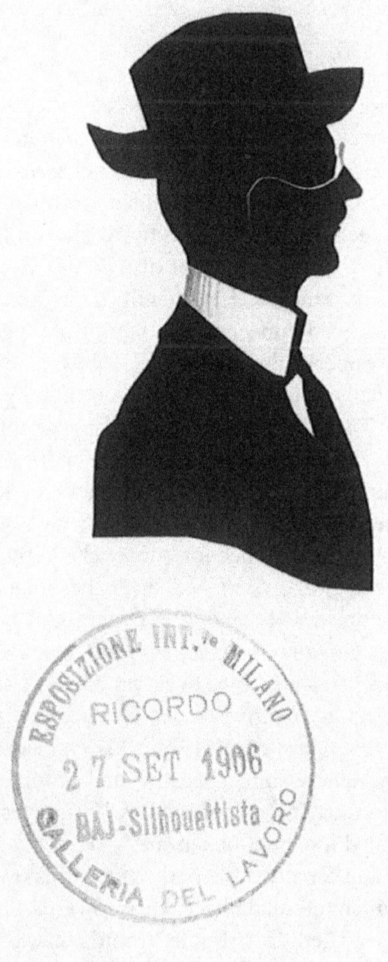

Figure 7.5 A souvenir from Milan, 1906

(Reproduced with the permission of the Blackburn Museum and Art Gallery)

termination of hostilities before the extension could take place by reducing the capital cost to the taxpayers in this way. Hart stated that he would like to make some contribution for the 'benefit of my native town.'[37] Mr Hindle concluded that 'Mr Hart was especially desirous that the matter should be kept secret. He left me with a cheque for £10,000.'[38] Hart's collection of books was not assembled with the same motivation as Lord Brotherton of Leeds, who aspired to create a 'Bodleian of the North.' Hart's smaller but extremely high-quality collection of books and coins were to be left, not as a national treasure, but specifically to the inhabitants of his local town of Blackburn. This was a highly developed regionalism, distinct from a service to the nation.

Hart's clear intentions for his specific bequests were reflective of the Christian values central to the new industrialist class to which he and his family belonged. His activities as an agent for the perceived public good of his community were specific to the betterment of lives through the salvation of souls through Christian conversion, the protection of children through his work for the Blackburn Orphanage and the improvement of education through his work as a trustee of the Blackburn Grammar School as a representative of the University of Manchester. With regard to his lifelong passion for collecting, it may be that he believed that the rarity and beauty of the books and coins he collected could also act as agents of betterment and change. Amy Woudson-Boulton has argued that the 'Victorians evinced a great belief in the didactic and morally transformative potential of objects, whether art or natural specimens, even as mass production was revolutionizing labour relations, consumption patterns, the domestic environment, and traditional practices of all kinds.'[39] The power of physical collections with their capacity to fascinate and move the observer would have been well understood by Hart and his contemporaries. Arthur Bowdler wrote of his coleoptera collection that 'no jewel ever flashed and blazed with greater brilliance than some of these gems which are among the despised of the earth.'[40] The final aim for regional collectors of Hart's time and social class would have been the enhancing gift to their communities, regardless of the personal pleasure accrued during the collecting process. The choice to reside in the communities where their industries were based, albeit removed from the intensely crowded conditions of the town, must have influenced the focus of philanthropic activity for these Blackburnian industrial elite.

In his journal of 1856, weaver John O'Neil recorded that on 8 October, he and his friend Richard Wrigley walked from Clitheroe to Blackburn for the market day, a distance of 21 miles in total, a four-hour walk in each direction. Although O'Neil was impressed with the variety of goods for sale in the Blackburn market, he was unimpressed with the town itself. He wrote, 'I had never been in Blackburn before and now after I had seen it all through I think little of it. It is the poorest looking place of a large town that I have ever seen, there is no buildings of any importance except the Town Hall which has just been built and is not quite finished yet.'[41] O'Neil's diary entry gives the impression of a town in the midst of great change in the process of accommodating its seismic shift in population and culture. Many of those who profited most from this transformation, the cotton masters and their fellow industrialists, would strive to change it from within, through investment in cultural capital in the form of the bequest, something 'for my native town.'

Conclusion

The motivations behind R. E. Hart's collecting were significantly different from those of wealthy British and North American collectors like Alfred Chester Beatty, the Morgans and Sir Thomas Phillipps.[42] Whereas they aimed at national and even international recognition for their collections and also for their personal achievements in collecting, Hart's audience was much more specific, and his aims were much more community oriented. His collections, although much smaller, were intended to become a regional treasure, which would benefit the inhabitants of Blackburn into the future. His collecting was one way in which he demonstrated the Christian values of the industrialist class to which he belonged, and through which he could help to improve the lives of people in his specific community. His collections were part of a broader programme of philanthropy, designed to educate, better and enhance the community in which he chose to reside.

Notes

1 See Mike Rothwell's listings of associated textile industries in *Industrial Heritage: A Guide to the Industrial Archaeology of Blackburn* (Hyndburn: Hyndburn Local History Society, 1986), pp. 35–39.
2 See Robert Edward Hart's publication on the mechanical engineering of the Lambeth Power Rope in *Rope Driving or the Transmission of Power by Ropes* (Blackburn: Thomas Hart Ltd., 1909).
3 See note of Thomas Hindle, Town Clerk, 12 July 1944, who quotes a statement of R. E. Hart with regard to the bequest of his collections to the Blackburn Public Library. (Blackburn Museum and Art Gallery, R. E. Hart archives).
4 Giles Waterfield, *The People's Museums, Art Museums and Exhibitions in Britain, 1800–1914* (New Haven and London: Yale University Press, 2015), especially Chapter 4, 'Promising Soil: The Cities of the Industrial Revolution and the Earliest Civic Art Galleries,' pp. 65–85.
5 Cynthia Johnston and Jack Hartnell, eds., *Cotton to Gold, Extraordinary Collections of the Industrial North West* (Exhibition Catalogue) (London: Two Temple Place, 2015), pp. 36–37.

6 Derek Beattie, *Blackburn, the Development of a Lancashire Cotton Town* (Halifax: Ryburn Publishing Ltd., 1992), pp. 11–28.
7 Henry Bannerman & Sons, *The Diary and Buyers' Guide* (Manchester: Henry Bannerman & Sons, 1897), pp. 77–81 (at p. 78).
8 *Ibid.*
9 *Ibid.*, p. 79.
10 *Ibid.*
11 The writer comments that the produce of the Blackburn looms would 'include almost every form of cotton-woven fabrics.' The most popular fabrics are the 'Blackburn greys' made of a mixture of cotton and linen. The 'greys' are woven without the yarns being dyed. The fabric is then sent to London for printing (p. 80).
12 Beattie, *Blackburn*, Chapter 3, 'Elites and Political Power before 1914,' pp. 29–48.
13 *Ibid.*, p. 31.
14 *Ibid.*
15 Anthony Howe, *The Cotton Masters, 1830–1860* (Oxford: Clarendon Press, 1984), pp. 310–315 (at p. 310).
16 Beattie argues that 'with no local aristocracy to model themselves on, these families developed their own social mores more attuned to their new class position and often based on an idealised but modest country gentry' (p. 32).
17 Howe, *Cotton Masters*, p. 315.
18 Henry Whittaker, *The Union Club, Blackburn 1849–1949, a Short History* (Blackburn: J. Dickinson & Sons, 1950), p. 7.
19 *Ibid.*, pp. 6–7.
20 *Ibid.*, p. 7.
21 *Ibid.*, p. 150.
22 Howe, *Cotton Masters*, p. 315.
23 Mike Rothwell, *Industrial Heritage: A Guide to the Industrial Archaeology of Blackburn* (Hyndburn: Hyndburn Local History Society, 1986), pp. 36–37.
24 *Ibid.*, p. 36.
25 John George Shaw, *History of Thomas Hart's Rope Works, Blackburn* (Blackburn, 1930).
26 For the history of the founding of the Blackburn Orphanage see Melanie Warren, *James Dixon's Children* (Lancaster: Fleetwood Books, 2013).
27 R. E. Hart's school reports from both Horace Hill and Rugby School are held by the Blackburn Museum and Art Gallery.
28 David Newland, '125 Years of Cambridge Engineering,' *Cambridge, the Magazine of the Cambridge Society*, 47 (2001), 11–18.
29 *Ibid.*, 11.
30 College Order of 1 August 1944 records that the £10,000 was given 'as a mark of affectionate esteem for his old College, to be expended as thought best.'
31 See the description by J. C. T. Oates of the Hart bequest of 1946 in *A Catalogue of Fifteenth-Century Books in the Cambridge University Library* (Cambridge: Cambridge University Press, 1954), p. 49.
32 Maurice Ettinghausen, *Rare Books and Royal Collectors: Memoirs of an Antiquarian Bookseller* (New York: Simon and Shuster, 1966), pp. 74–75.
33 Robert Graves, *Goodbye to All That* (London: Jonathan Cape, 1929, rept. Penguin Books, 1960, 2000), pp. 21–22.
34 *Ibid.*

35 Note by Thomas Hindle, Blackburn Town Clerk, 12 July 1944, quoting the statement of R. E. Hart with regard to the bequest of his collections to the Blackburn Public Library (Blackburn Museum and Art Gallery, R. E. Hart archives).
36 Cynthia A. Johnston and Sarah J. Biggs, eds., *Blackburn's Worthy Citizen: The Philanthropic Legacy of R. E. Hart* (Exhibition Catalogue) (London: Institute of English Studies, 2013, rept. 2014 and 2016).
37 Hindle, note of 12 July 1944.
38 *Ibid.*
39 Amy Woudson-Boulton, *Transformative Beauty: Art Museums in Industrial Britain* (Stanford: Stanford University Press, 2012), p. 16.
40 Arthur Bowdler in *The Blackburn Telegraph*, 1908.
41 John O'Neil, *A Lancashire Weaver's Journal, 1856–1864, 1872–1875*, vol. 122, ed. by Mary Brigg (Manchester: The Record Society of Lancashire and Cheshire, 1981), p. 22.
42 See the chapters by Laura Cleaver and Danielle Magnusson and Toby Burrows in this volume.

8 Ossified collections

The past encapsulated in British institutions today

Karen Attar

'Floreat bibliomania' was the title given by A. N. L. Munby, that great student of collecting, to an article published in the *New Statesman* on 21 June 1952.[1] Munby's main interest was in sale catalogues as records of books assembled and then dispersed.[2] This chapter provides an overview of a more philanthropic and stable end to collecting: collections primarily of printed books in the British Isles that have stayed together and now enrich institutions, causing broader swathes of scholars and librarians to echo Munby's prayer. Whilst some outstanding collectors and bibliophiles are highlighted in the chapters in this volume and in the standard literature of collecting, and other more modest ones are noted in magisterial histories of institutions, are featured in dedicated articles or are commemorated in published catalogues of their collections, they still form only a minority of the huge numbers of collectors who have donated books to institutional collections in the nineteenth and twentieth centuries.[3]

This overview takes a look at what has been described as 'the rest of the iceberg,' through a survey of 873 repositories in the British Isles: national, academic, school, public, subscription and professional libraries, or in trusts, cathedrals, churches, monasteries, London clubs, archives, museums, schools, companies and stately homes.[4] Discussing popular collecting subjects and trends in collecting, the survey concentrates on 'collections' as groups of books with some unifying element, most of which originated with an individual before entering corporate ownership, whilst retaining at least some semblance of their former identity.

These 'ossified' collections are not necessarily complete libraries. Some were incomplete at the point of entering institutional care, having previously undergone erosions through theft, war damage or, particularly, sales.[5] Especially prone to this kind of fate are noblemen's collections in stately homes, now largely National Trust properties: for example, the libraries of the bibliomaniac and man of letters Isaac D'Israeli (1766–1848) at Hughenden in High Wycombe; of William Blathwayt (1649?–1717), Minister at War to

William III, at Dyrham Park, near Bath; and of the early family collection of the Paget family, Marquesses of Anglesey, at Beaudesert (now housed in Plas Newydd in Anglesey), to provide instances of far-flung library remnants with diverse former owners.[6] But non-aristocratic collections are also affected, and more modest libraries which exist only as fractions of their former selves include those of the poet and theologian Isaac Williams (1802–1865; a prominent member of the Oxford Movement) at Lampeter, now in academic ownership, and of the photographic pioneer William Henry Fox Talbot (1800–1877) and of George Bernard Shaw, as well as the remains at Gloucester Cathedral of a school library covering all subjects begun by clergyman Maurice Wheeler (1647/8–1727), Master of the College School 1684–1712.[7]

Sometimes owners deliberately split their libraries, such as the eighteenth-century antiquarian Jacob Bryant (1715–1804), who bequeathed most of his books to King's College Cambridge (Eton having disgruntled him by wanting him to pay for the transport), but excepted divinity, travel and the books in the glass case in his best chamber, having already given away his Caxtons, and Edward Worth (1678–1733), who when leaving most of his books to Dr Steevens's Hospital in Dublin diverted some of the best on English literature to Clotilda, Lady Eustace.[8] The most striking instance of a collection scattered between institutions is the Shakespeare-related material gathered by the Shakespearean scholar James Orchard Halliwell-Phillipps (1820–1889): whilst Edinburgh University Library claims to have the bulk of his literary collection (approximately 1,600 items, including some early Shakespeare quartos), further material is to be found at Brighton & Hove City Libraries, the Penzance Library, Chetham's Library in Manchester and the Shakespeare Birthplace Trust in Stratford upon Avon.[9]

Alternatively, the division of discrete collections assembled by an individual may be institutional, as when in 1950 London's Guildhall relinquished two very different collections assembled by Edward Phelips (1882–1928), passing some 3,500 early printed books pertaining to Spain, especially the urban history of Madrid, to the University of London, and erotica to the British Library.[10] Institutional libraries may also have dispersed parts of collections, as in 1947 Chichester Cathedral did with some of the library of Bishop Henry King (1592–1669),[11] or cherry-picked from collections, as King's College Cambridge did with the collection of Provost George Thackeray (1777–1850), the bulk of which his daughter bequeathed to the college in 1879.[12]

Collection focuses

Early in the nineteenth century, Thomas Frognall Dibdin noted a bibliophilic desire for illustration and beautiful books alongside early printing, areas which have proved to be long-standing attractions. As John Carter wrote, 'The collecting of early printed books, fine bindings and the masterpieces of typography and illustration of all periods continued strongly during the last quarter of the nineteenth century, as it continues today.'[13] Although fashionable topics for book collections over the past two centuries have been noted, 'collectible' books can, according to A. W. Pollard's classic definition, be anything that appeals to the mind, the eye, or the imagination: in other words, collections can be based around anything at all.[14] Those ossified in institutional libraries reflect the great variety of subject matter, from artillery to bagpipes, Miss Great Britain and the Titanic, covering food and drink, all sorts of sports and pastimes, railways and travel more widely, medicine and the natural sciences and the fine arts among other subjects.[15] French drama and playbills, not noted by the theorists, recur.[16] Some subjects may seem obvious, such as the numerous collections devoted to Bibles, liturgies and hymnologies, long identified as popular collecting areas and meeting desires both for beauty and cultural significance.[17] Others are less so. For example, no fewer than 11 special collections in the United Kingdom focus on shorthand, in collections of varying sizes that partly overlap in timespan and are partly complementary. The Dickens scholar and shorthand bibliographer William J. Carlton (1886–1973) assembled the largest and most comprehensive at London's Senate House Library: an estimated 18,000 books, periodicals and pamphlets on all aspects of stenography from the sixteenth to the twentieth centuries, of all countries and systems in nearly 60 languages and dialects. No lesser a person in the field than Sir Isaac Pitman (1813–1897) and his grandson, Sir James Pitman (1901–1985), assembled a shorthand collection of 4,000 volumes from the seventeenth to the late twentieth centuries (University of Bath), whilst the Scottish Esperantist John Mabon Warden (1856–1933), Vice-President of the Esperantista Akademio, collected about 4,600 items, mostly from the nineteenth and twentieth centuries, about or in hundreds of systems of shorthand and presented them to the National Library of Scotland. The National Library of Wales, the Mitchell Library in Glasgow, and six more English libraries hold further collections.

Conversely, one may expect subjects to be ubiquitous that in fact are not. The Royal Family may seem an obvious collecting subject with the production of conscious memorabilia, but this has infiltrated at an institutional, permanent level only with the Kimber Collection given in the 1990s to the University of Leeds: 1,255 works, including many newspaper and magazine special editions to commemorate notable royal events, mostly from 1930 to 1996, relating to the British monarchy, especially individual members of the Royal Family.[18]

Civil War pamphlets occur across the United Kingdom, across a range of repositories, ecclesiastical, academic, public and private, ranging from

Trinity College, Cambridge and a school, Dulwich College, to the Leeds Library (a subscription library), Lord Lonsdale's pamphlets at Cumbria Archives and Local Studies Centre in Barrow-in-Furness, and to the Twistleton-Wykeham-Fiennes family books at Broughton Castle, Banbury. Among the more significant collections are over 1,000 tracts at the London School of Economics, mostly from a collection of unspecified origin purchased in 1932; about 2,000 at York Minster given by the nineteenth-century local solicitor Edward Hailstone as part of a 10,000-item strong collection supposed to have been the most extensive series of works relating to Yorkshire ever brought together; and collections at Exeter Cathedral and Worcester County Council, based on a bequest by Worcester bookseller John Grainger in 1900. Unlike author or publisher collections (see later), which must by their nature overlap, the Civil War collections are to an extent complementary and local, a sobering reminder through print culture of the pervasiveness of the war. Not only is the aforementioned collection at York Minster part of a collection pertaining to Yorkshire, but Civil War pamphlets and tracts in the Essex Society for Archaeology & History Library, held at the University of Essex, relate to Colchester and its siege in 1648; a small collection at Reading Central Library is in its Local Studies Library; a collection at the Great North Museum in Newcastle from the Society of Antiquaries of Newcastle upon Tyne Library relates mainly to Civil War activities in northern England; those in the Bradshaw Collection at Newcastle University also mostly describe local events; and a clutch at Senate House Library is part of Alfred Claude Bromhead's collection pertaining to the history of London.

Collections of children's books, noted by Percy Muir as a phenomenon of the first half of the twentieth century, are very common.[19] Forty-three (5%) of the 873 repositories in the *Directory of Rare Book and Special Collections in the United Kingdom and Republic of Ireland* have collections of children's books, and those are merely the libraries which include the specific phrase 'children's books' in the description; there are certainly more. Even a small collection of children's books can include rare or unique editions, as, not being inherently academic, they are not the staple of the libraries that are the chief preservers of books. Personal collectors may be attracted both by nostalgia and by affordability: the price, ten pence, is still pencilled in some books in a small collection of late Victorian prize books at Senate House Library, assembled and given in the late 1970s or early 1980s by former Librarian J. H. P. Pafford. They offer a wide collecting scope. Like the Civil War pamphlets, a local interest may be discernible: early children's books in Welsh as part of a 10,000-item strong Welsh collection at the Central Library in Cardiff, and approximately 500 Welsh children's books from the nineteenth and early twentieth centuries, assembled by writer and schoolmaster D. J. Williams (1886–1950) and given by him to the National Library of Wales at Aberystwyth; a children's collection of about 4,000 volumes, chiefly pre-1939, often with a Scottish connection, at the Mitchell Library in Glasgow. The collections can be primarily of fiction, or of textbooks. They can be thematic, such as a group of 668 books from the eighteenth to twentieth centuries at Leo Baeck College in London of books for and about Jewish children collected by Charles Barry Hyams and Helge-Ulrike Hyams, founders of a museum of childhood at Marburg and (Helge-Ulrike) author of *German Jewish Children's Books, 1667–1938* (Montreal: Goethe Institute, 2000); these are balanced more chillingly by German National Socialist books written for children (see n. 52). A couple of collections focus on a single title. England sports two *Alice in Wonderland* collections, over 130 copies in many languages and featuring a multitude of illustrators at Homerton College in Cambridge, and a collection at Lewis Carroll's Oxford college, Christ Church; an illustrated books collection at Middlesex University also mentions having *Alice* in several editions. In 2004 Brian Baker bequeathed to the University of Reading a collection of about 800 volumes based around L. Frank Baum's *Wizard of Oz* (one of few American-based collections in the United Kingdom): editions and translations, sequels by other authors, and other books by Baum, some written pseudonymously.

Single title collections extend beyond childrens' books. Editions of *De Imitatione Christi*, attributed to Thomas à Kempis and included in William Carew Hazlitt's list of collecting subjects at the turn of the twentieth century, constitute the focus of three institutional collections, at least two of which were formed at that time. Two are modest, 98 items collected by Rayner Storr (1835–1917, compiler of the work's concordance), now at Dr Williams's Library, and 140 items collected by the statistician George Udny Yule (1871–1951), held at St John's College, Cambridge. The collection at the British Library based on the antiquary Edward Waterton's (1830–1887), however, comprises 1,014 editions and is probably the country's largest single title collection.[20] The *Eikon Basilike*, a logical offshoot of Civil War collecting, is a subject of more collections; however, three of the four collections based around it emanate from one person, its bibliographer Francis Falconer Madan.[21] Collections devoted to a single author – usually but not invariably a literary one – are common, from Castiglione, Dante, the Brontës, and Dickens to Catherine Cookson, Iris Murdoch and Graham Greene.[22] Particular authors can increase in collecting prominence: 20 years ago, Bromley Public Libraries held the only collection devoted to the poet Walter de la Mare (provenance not noted).[23] By 2015 two more had joined it: 325 items collected by Phyllis T. M. Davies now at Cambridge University, and de la Mare's own working library (almost 700 items) with his family's collection of editions of his works (some 420 titles), at Senate House Library, University of London.[24]

Also common is local topography, recommended at the First Annual Meeting of the Library Association in October 1878 by William Henry Kearley Wright as material which provincial libraries should endeavour to collect: 'Efforts should be made to collect therein all useful books, pamphlets, or manuscripts having any connexion with the district, whether descriptive of, relating to, published in, or written by natives of, or sometimes residents within the limits of such district.'[25] Such collections are not exclusive to public libraries, albeit most common there, and are sometimes based on the collections of individuals.[26]

Awareness of local interest at country and town level emerges strongly in collections based around individuals. All three repositories across the British Isles devoted to W. B. Yeats are, for example, in the Republic of Ireland, whilst all four collections based around the Langholm-born poet, essayist, journalist and political figure Hugh MacDiarmid (1892–1978) are in Scotland, and the two collections devoted to the social reformer Robert Owen are exclusively in his native Wales.[27] Although Robert Burns has been adopted as a 'British' poet – Quiller Couch included him in *The Oxford Book of English Verse* – three of the four Burns collections in the *Directory*, of between 2,000 and 7,000 volumes each, are in his native Scotland, in Dunfermline, Glasgow and at his home in Ayr.[28] Even Sir Walter Scott, whose popularity transcended all boundaries, is all but limited to his native land as regards special collections, most spectacularly the bulk of the Abbotsford Library, the books Scott owned (over 8,500 volumes) at the Advocates' Library in Edinburgh; approximately 7,000 volumes from the eighteenth to the twentieth centuries by and about Scott acquired by his bibliographer James Corson (1905–1988), former Deputy Librarian of Edinburgh University Library, at Edinburgh University Library; and about 6,000 volumes at Aberdeen University Library, from editions, translations and secondary literature to adaptations, ranging from operatic libretti to comic strips.[29] All four collections on the wood engraver Thomas Bewick are in his home territory of Northumberland. At the city level, all three special collections in the United Kingdom devoted specifically to Dylan Thomas are in his native Swansea: in the University there, the Museum, and Swansea Central Library. Two of the three repositories with collections devoted to John Bunyan, identified in the early twentieth century as generally collectible,[30] are in his native Bedford; three of the four collections centred around Elizabeth Gaskell are held where she lived in Knutsford and Manchester; Great Britain' s sole collection of P. G. Wodehouse books (almost 3,000 items) is at his old school, Dulwich College and so forth.[31] As another aspect of the local theme, very few collections are based around any non-British writers beyond the Renaissance: apart from L. Frank Baum, noted previously, only Walt Whitman and Rainer Maria Rilke stand out.[32]

Local interest at national and city level extends beyond individual people to specific subjects. Scottish-related collections, for example, include about 1,500 volumes of Celtica amassed by Sir Robert Gordon of Letterfourie (1824–1908) now held at the Sabhal Mòr Ostaig Library on Skye; the Wighton Collection of 620 volumes of chiefly Scottish national music at Dundee Central Library, bequeathed by Dundee grocer and town councillor Andrew John Wighton (1804–1866); and around 100 books with bindings designed by Talwin Morris (1865–1911), art director for the Glasgow publishing firm Blackie & Son at a time when the 'Glasgow style' was gaining momentum, in Glasgow University Library. Whilst Arthurian romances will be found everywhere, the two special collections of Arthurian literature in the United Kingdom are in Wales, at the National Library of Wales and in the Arthurian Centre at Bangor University.[33] National relevance can be more obscure. The draughts enthusiast James Hillhouse (d. 1928), President of the Scottish Draughts Association, collected books on the game of draughts (371 volumes) which the Mitchell Library in Glasgow purchased in 1878; this may seem to be just one aspect of the numerous collections in the British Isles on leisure activities, but in fact reflects Scottish domination of the game at the time.[34]

Early printing is well represented in institutional collections – which, however, do not fully reflect personal collecting patterns. The literature of bibliophilia paired Aldines with Elzeviers, with the physician and poet John Ferriar (1761–1815) writing:

> The folio-Aldus loads your happy shelves,
> And dapper Elzevirs, like fairy elves,
> Shew their light forms amidst the well-gilt Twelves.[35]

Andrew Lang in 1886 wrote: 'It is a point of sentiment to like books just as they left the hands of the old printers – of Estienne, Aldus, or Louis Elzevir.'[36] In some institutional collections the two publishing dynasties of cheap classical textbooks remain paired, such as in the collections given to the Bodleian Library by the Dante scholar Paget Jackson Toynbee (1855–1932), to Newcastle University by the classical scholar G. B. A. Fletcher (1903–1995), and to Dublin by the eighteenth-century Dublin physician Edward Worth (1676–1733).[37] Yet while past Elzevier collections are known,[38] Aldines dwarf Elzeviers in preserved ones. Elzeviers as the single major collection focus are present institutionally only through the collection of one H. Beaumont, who in 1900 offered his collection of some 700 Elzevier publications and 400 other examples of seventeenth-century Dutch printing to London's Guildhall.[39] Aldines, by contrast, were collected by the nineteenth-century bibliophiles Lord Spencer and Richard Copley Christie, with the result that the John Rylands Library now has an Aldine Collection of 2,000 volumes. The Lincolnshire baronet and classical scholar Sir Richard Ellys of Nocton (1682–1742) had many in a collection which demonstrates interest in early printing, now at Blickling Hall;[40] Aldines collected by the headmaster and clergyman Matthew Raine (1760–1811) and bequeathed by his brother Jonathan are a strength at Trinity College, Cambridge;[41] and L. O. Bigg collected 160 Aldines in Italy which his brother gave to Harrow School.

Collectors in the twentieth century and beyond retained the idea of collecting the output of particular publishers and extended the boundaries beyond early printers. Penguin books are particularly popular. The largest collection, an estimated 28,000 volumes at the University of Bristol comprising founder Allen Lane's personal copies of Penguin's output, is complemented by several smaller ones, such as the 359-volume set of Penguin Specials collected by Stuart James, a former Librarian of the University of the West of Scotland, and about 3,500 books collected by Angus Mitchell, a Chair of the University of Stirling court, given to the collectors' respective universities in Scotland. William B. Todd (1919–2011) with his wife and co-researcher Ann Bowden (1924–2001), and Dr Karl H. Pressler (1926–2009), with a collection augmented by Michael Kahan, collected Tauchnitz books, which passed to the British Library (1992) and the National Library of Scotland (2011) respectively.[42] Local interest extends to publisher collections. Both Birmingham Public Library and Birmingham University hold almost complete collections of Baskerville books, the latter stemming from the mid-twentieth-century gift of the brother of the Birmingham professor Victor Hely-Hutchinson. The University of Reading holds the Two Rivers Press Collection, the ongoing output of a firm which produces books in and about Reading, and about 2,000 nineteenth-century books from the MacLehose Press in Glasgow are at Glasgow University Library.

Collections pertaining to particular publishers merge with a long-standing focus on collecting beautiful books in numerous collections of private press books, whether of particular presses, especially William Morris's Kelmscott Press, or of private presses more widely.[43] William Ridler (1909–1980) of Kings Norton may well have amassed the largest general private press collection, of over 3,440 private press books (mainly British) and other examples of fine printing, now at the Library of Birmingham.[44] Among others, Joseph Pomfret (1878–1944), a former librarian of Preston Harris Library in Lancashire, donated to it about 600 volumes from various private presses, and the engraver, printer and typographical adviser Sir Emery

Walker (1851–1933) amassed some thousand books and trial pages from the earlier days of the private press movement, purchased in 1990 by Cheltenham's Art Gallery & Museum.[45]

Elsewhere the specific aspects have been fragmented, as in collections of illustrated books, such as the twentieth-century collections made by Lord Fairhaven, at Anglesey Abbey, and by Graham Watson, given to Emmanuel College, Cambridge.[46] Permutations of the form are present, for example, with collections of miniature books, of which Edward Arnold (d. 1823?) and Ursula Mary Radford (1894–1976) formed the largest personal collections, of 100 and over 300 books respectively.[47] The appeal of 'the book beautiful,' reduced to the outside of books, is ossified in collections devoted to bindings. Of these, the Henry Davis collection of 889 bindings primarily from Britain and Europe at the British Library has the greatest profile through catalogues and other publications devoted to it.[48] The largest is the diplomat Charles Ramsden's (1888–1958) collection of 1,500 English and French bindings, dated from 1780 to 1840, also at the British Library. Smaller collections are devoted to single binders or types of bindings, such as the 965 British armorial bindings from the sixteenth to the nineteenth centuries assembled by Henry Clements (1869–1940) and given to the Victoria and Albert Museum, art bindings in various styles by solicitor and amateur binder Alvah Cook (b. 1865) at Bath Central Library,[49] and the Hanson collection at the Bodleian Library devoted to the Edwards family of Halifax, some of whose distinctive bindings (following the local motif) are also held in two public libraries at Halifax.[50]

Why collect?

The perennial personal desires for illustration and beautiful books alongside early printing, recorded by Dibdin, are well preserved institutionally. Lord Spencer, whose collection at the base of the John Rylands Library, Manchester, was known intimately to Dibdin, is an obvious example. Samuel Sandars (1837–1894) is another, accumulating 1,460 volumes from the fifteenth century onwards including 'liturgies, early English printing, books on vellum, fine bindings, 109 incunabula'; the Liverpool merchant Hugh Frederick Hornby (1826–1899) a third.[51]

A desire to preserve the past begins with the antiquarian collections of the sixteenth century onwards, strongly evinced in the collections of such well-known figures as Matthew Parker (1504–1575) at Corpus Christi College, Cambridge and Robert Cotton (1571–1631) at the British Library, whose gathering of material objects formed another aspect of the commemoration of the past demonstrated by Parker's contemporaries, the antiquaries John Bale (1495–1653) and John Leland (c. 1503–1552), through documentary activity. Preservation of the past moves into collection of the present: the collecting of newly published items, possibly ephemeral, by men conscious of living in momentous times which would become historically significant, from the English Civil War to the First World War.[52] As in the sixteenth century, amassing tangible items is just one facet of the desire to record, a wish expressed in another form by Mass Observation's encouragement to write diaries and respond to surveys during the Second World War.[53] The individual gains significance through his alignment with major events. Briefer events may also be commemorated, such as the Great Exhibition of 1851.[54] An offshoot may be the desire to preserve the culture of one's time, whether turbulent or not, seen famously in the seventeenth-century examples of George Thomason's tracts at the British Library and Samuel Pepys's collection of broadside ballads at Magdalene College, Cambridge.[55] Identification with place rather than time as a motivating factor emerges in those collections pertaining to the topography or eminent inhabitants of the collectors' local areas.

The dividing line between collecting for the pleasure of the activity or possession and acquiring books for use is blurred: a group of utilitarian books can become a collection and a collection can be put to use, as when collectors have produced bibliographies based at least partly on their collections, perhaps most prolifically the surgeon and bibliographer Geoffrey Keynes with his books about, and bibliographies on, Jane Austen, John Donne, Rupert Brooke and William Harvey among others.[56] Bibliophilia and research combine in other instances. The economic historian Herbert Somerton Foxwell (1849–1936), a compulsive collector of books and pamphlets on all areas of economics, began his collection of some 30,000 titles from the fifteenth century onwards (now at the University of London) with the intention of preparing a historical edition of Adam Smith's *Wealth of Nations*, and expanded from there.[57] One step below that is the amassing of books to back theories, as when the Baconian Sir Edwin Durning-Lawrence (1837–1914) gathered 'Baconian' books, especially from the seventeenth century, in order, as his widow explained, 'to prove that Francis Bacon was at the head of a great literary and scientific society, from whence emanated all the Elizabethan and Jacobean literature'; she explicitly noted that he was not a bibliophile.[58] Scholars' working libraries of primarily modern works can contain antiquarian books: for example, the 500-item strong library on Quakers and other subjects at University College Cork assembled by Richard S. Harrison, author of books on Irish Quakers, includes 90 books from the seventeenth and eighteenth centuries among the later volumes. The fairly recent but constantly accelerating phenomenon of scholarly access to digital surrogates of pre-twentieth-century books could lead in future to readier differentiation between 'collections' and 'working libraries,' as scholars will not require earlier books on their physical shelves for purely utilitarian textual purposes.[59]

Standard working libraries from a distant age that have been kept together automatically gain the status of 'collections' in public institutions, such as the 230 or so medical books from the sixteenth to the eighteenth centuries of the medical man James Simson (1740–1770) at St Andrews University Library. Many more recent working libraries of scholars or of significant literary or social figures, the contents of which are not intrinsically rare, gain significance as special collections when they enter the public sphere by virtue of their immediate provenance, sometimes enhanced by the annotations of their former owners.[60] Typical among these are the working libraries of Sigmund Freud and his daughter Anna at the Freud Museum in London; of Sir John Betjeman at Exeter University Library; of the philosopher of religion Baron Friedrich von Hügel (1852–1925) at St Andrews University; and of papyrologist Sir Idris Bell (1879–1967) at the National Library of Wales, to name just a few libraries which demonstrate a broad sweep of subjects and of location.[61]

Ossified collections embody the manifold reasons motivating private collectors. Yet even when kept intact and unaltered, personal collections change their meaning when they enter institutions, to serve further institutional aims. Institutions prove their endorsement of the subjects of private bibliophilic enthusiasms by adding to them their own special collections in the same areas. Several institutions have sought actively to acquire, or have segregated, the output of private presses as special collections, as seen in private press collections at Brighton & Hove City Libraries (over 600 volumes), at Manchester Central Library (1,700 volumes), within the Librarian's Collection at St Andrews University Library (about 1,500 books in all), and the Kelmscott Press Collection at the National Library of Scotland.[62] They have frequently collocated their incunabula (although there are also practical reasons for doing this) and have brought together their own collections of miniature or (at the London Library) little books; the Mitchell Library in Glasgow is noteworthy for an ongoing collection of miniature books from the early seventeenth to the twenty-first centuries, featuring books from the local publishers David Bryce & Son (Glasgow) and the Gleniffer Press (Paisley and Wigtown).[63] Beautiful books, in the form of artists' books, have been brought together as special collections by institutions for which they are relevant rather than having been amassed and passed on from individuals.[64] But the bibliophilic enjoyment which may have motivated the personal owner is largely replaced by research value and use, although the visual appeal remains useful for advocacy and marketing, in exhibitions, and to impress donors.

Whilst institutions encapsulate levels of history by representing permanently within their special collections the various changing fashions of personal collecting, they simultaneously muffle history through the loss of immediacy of the 'now' collection. Even if the event with which the personal collector has identified remains current at the time of institutional acquisition (which is unlikely), it will soon lose currency in the corporate context. Identification with place, on the other hand, remains as relevant corporately as personally, institutions may strengthen it by aggregating such collections. A prime example is the University of Bradford, two-thirds of whose 17 named special collections are connected in some way with Bradford or Yorkshire, in a department which describes the special collections as 'reflecting the story of the University and the City.'[65] Institutions sometimes choose to emphasize local interest by retaining donations by an author as special collections, such as books by G. A. Henty bequeathed by him to Westminster School, where he was educated, and Eleanor Farjeon's gift of her works to the public library in Hampstead, where she lived.[66] Such local collections differentiate repositories from each other, bolstering desires to be 'unique and distinctive' and gain validation and status thereby.[67]

Women and collections

A. N. L. Munby declared loftily that women did not collect books.[68] Exceptions can prove the rule: Miriam Robinette Tomkinson (1916–1986) bequeathed incunabula and books emanating from the great sixteenth-century scholar-printers among others to the Bodleian Library, and the core of the Romany collection for which the University of Leeds is famous (over 650 books and pamphlets in addition to manuscript material, artefacts and ephemera) was assembled by Dorothy Una McGrigor Phillipps.[69] But the evidence of collections within institutional libraries shows collecting indeed to be male dominated:[70] hardly surprisingly, as income for many centuries was centred in male hands. The earliest female collector whose books have been preserved institutionally is, significantly, noble: the literary patron Anne Sadleir (1575–1671/2), eldest daughter of Sir Edward Coke, who bequeathed her (mostly devotional) books to the Inner Temple. Female collectors (as distinct from owners, where the two can be distinguished) tend to be seen from the late nineteenth century onwards. They are often professional, so have means, and their working interests may overlap with the collecting one, seen in the collections of academics[71] and of women in creative fields, such as the food writers Prue Leith and Jane Grigson, now at Oxford Brookes University,[72] the pianist and composer Joan Trimble (1915–2000), who gave 1,000 music scores and books to the Royal Irish Academy of Music and the singer Rita Williams, who gave about 3,000 popular songs from the 1920s onwards to the Trinity Laban Conservatoire. The collections are often modest in size, numbering fewer than 500 volumes, although there are exceptions: Williams's and Grigson's collections are two, and the most voluminous collection made by a single woman is probably Melissa Hardie-Budden's Hypatia Collection at Exeter University, 10,000 items from the twentieth century by or about women.[73] The largest female-related collections were formed by two husband and wife teams, collecting children's books and related materials from the sixteenth to the twentieth centuries: Peter and Iona Opie (about 20,000 items, now at the Bodleian Library), and Fernand and Anne Renier (some 80,000 books donated, with related material, to the Victoria and Albert Museum).[74] In other male-female teams, brother and sister Oliver and Marjory Wardrop collected Georgian books, now at the Bodleian Library, and the psychiatrists Ida Macalpine (1899–1974) and her son Richard Hunter, who also published books together, collected 7,000 works from the sixteenth to the nineteenth century on psychology, now at Cambridge University Library.[75]

Like men, women have collected a wide range of subjects, from early editions of Dante to Dada and Dundee.[76] Yet certain themes stand out. The typical domestic subjects tend to have been collected by women: the food and drink collections mentioned, and the only recorded collection devoted to needlework.[77] A number of women, like the aforenamed Joan Trimble and Rita Williams, collected music, notably Dorothea Ruggles-Brise (1866–1937), an expert on Scottish traditional music whose collection of some 500 books and manuscripts of early Scottish music is now at the A. K. Bell Library, a public library in Perth, Scotland.[78] Women collectors also have a certain predilection for children's books (generally modestly priced). For its sheer size and its range – over 10,500 items published between the seventeenth century and 1914 – Mary ('Paul') Pollard's collection at Trinity College Dublin stands out among these,[79] followed by 61.5 linear metres of eighteenth- and nineteenth-century children's books in English collected by Mary Thwaite and developed by Joan Butler, librarians in Hertfordshire, and 800 books in the Brunel University archives donated by Elsie Riach Murray (1861–1932), Vice-Principal of the Maria Grey Training College for Women Teachers.[80] All three collections of Charlotte M. Yonge's writings were formed by women, including Marghanita Laski, co-editor of the critical essays *A Chaplet for Charlotte Yonge*.[81] And although for its quantity and range the outstanding ephemera collection is John Johnson's in the Bodleian Library, women may also drift towards collecting ephemera, which is similarly doable on a low budget, on subjects as diverse as decorated papers, concert programmes and women's suffrage.[82]

Where women have been instrumental in preserving the past has been in passing on collections assembled by their male relatives. If one extends the concept of assembly to enabling, the prime example is Enriqueta Rylands, who with her husband's wealth was responsible for establishing the John Rylands Library in Manchester, including Lord Spencer's formidable collections of incunabula, Bibles, theology, Dantes and many other early printed works, and other collections.[83] But the generosity – or perhaps also the self-fulfilment, if women gave those collections as lasting memorials to the men they loved – covers collections in many places and sizes. The 1,500 comics, chiefly Disney productions, collected by the artist David Clarvis were bequeathed to the National Art Library of the Victoria and Albert Museum not by David Clarvis, but by his mother in 2003. The William Ridler collection of Fine Printing at the Library of Birmingham, mentioned previously, was deposited in 1988 by Ridler's wife, Ann. The Hawtin collection at University College Cork of 3,700 books on the Socialist Movement and economic history published during the formative years of the English Labour Party was bequeathed by Gillian Hawtin, including the library of her father, an early supporter of the Labour movement in London. The Baconian library of Baconian protagonist Sir Edwin Durning-Lawrence (approximately 5,750 items) was bequeathed to the University of London by his widow, Edith Jane. The list continues.

Conclusion

Where, finally, are we going with collecting the past? The first decades of the twenty-first century show satisfying activity. Admittedly dispersals have taken place, such as the loss of Joseph Mendham's (1769–1856) theological collection, rich in holdings from the fifteenth and sixteenth centuries, bequeathed to the Law Society and deposited at Canterbury Cathedral.[84] Yet there has also been major personal generosity, of old books as well as new, from a collection strong in French Revolutionary pamphlets given to Edinburgh University (2013) to author collections of T. S. Eliot and the Sitwells via books about Western perceptions of Russia printed between 1525 and 1917, and 2,120 books from the fifteenth to the twentieth century connected with the life and times of Michel de Montaigne among others.[85] An emphasis on machine-press books is increasing – at least partly perforce, as these constitute the majority of what is available. As the books collected become more modern, will the collections formed approximate more closely to existing institutional holdings, such that institutions will be reluctant to take collections in their areas of strength because there is a considerable level of duplication? Will institutions choose to preserve the collections that include more foreign books or more ephemeral books, as areas where the collector's books are likeliest to complement, rather than duplicate, an institution's holdings? Through libraries' selectivity, will the representation of fashions of collecting across the ages, the reliable ossification of the past, be weakened or even cease? Or will the emphasis change, with small libraries acquiring proportionately more special collections because of the reduced probability there of duplication? Time will tell.

Notes

1 Reprinted in A. N. L. Munby, *Essays and Papers*, ed. by Nicolas Barker (London: Scolar Press, 1977), pp. 37–41.

2 A. N. L. Munby, *Phillipps Studies*, 2 vols. (London: Sotheby Parke-Bernet, 1971), drawing together five separately published monographs about Sir Thomas Phillipps and his library (1951–1971); *British Book Sale Catalogues, 1676–1800: A Union List*, ed. by A. N. L. Munby and Lenore Coral (London: Mansell, 1977). See also the essay by Toby Burrows in this volume.

3 For staple works, both now quite old, describing salient book collectors, see Seymour de Ricci, *English Collectors of Books & Manuscripts (1530–1930) and Their Marks of Ownership* (Cambridge: Cambridge University Press, 1930; repr. New York: Burt Franklin, 1969; Bibliography and Reference Series, 268); William Younger Fletcher, *English Book Collectors* (The English Bookman's Library, 3) (London: K. Paul, Trench, Trübner, 1902; repr. New York: Burt Franklin, 1969; Bibliography and Reference Series, 209). Major institutional histories which deal with collectors are J. C. T. Oates, *Cambridge University Library: A History: From the Beginnings to the Copyright Act of Queen Anne*, David McKitterick, *Cambridge University Library: A History: The Eighteenth and Nineteenth Centuries* (both Cambridge: Cambridge University Press, 1986); P. R. Harris, *A History of the British Museum Library* (London: British Library, 1998); the British Library has also produced a book focussing on individual collectors and collections, *Libraries within the Library: The Origins of the British Library's Printed Collections*, ed. by Giles Mandelbrote and Barry Taylor (London: British Library, 2009). The major example of a published catalogue commemorating a collector, cited in booksellers' catalogues, is probably University of London Library, *Catalogue of the Goldsmiths' Library of Economic Literature*, compiled by Margaret Canney and David Knott, 5 vols. (London: Cambridge University Press, 1970–1995), although this catalogue contains many additions to the initial collection of Herbert Somerton Foxwell.

4 For the overview of 873 collections, see the *Directory of Rare Book and Special Collections in the United Kingdom and Republic of Ireland*, 3rd ed., ed. by Karen Attar (London: Facet Publishing, 2016). In some respects this article follows up David Pearson, 'Private Libraries and the Collecting Instinct,' in *The Cambridge History of Libraries in Britain and Ireland, vol. 3: 1850–2000*, ed. by Alistair Black and Peter Hoare (Cambridge: Cambridge University Press, 2006). The term 'the rest of the iceberg' was coined to describe nineteenth-century collections by Ed Potten, 'The Rest of the Iceberg: Reassessing Private Book Ownership in the Nineteenth Century,' in *Great Collectors and their Grand Designs: A*

Centenary Celebration of the Life and Work of A. N. L. Munby, ed. by Peter Murray Jones and Liam Sims, *Transactions of the Cambridge Bibliographical Society*, 15.3 (2014), 124–149.

5 The most salient example of sales from a public institution is the library of Sir Hans Sloane, one of the founding collections of the British Library. See, for example, Margaret A. E. Nickson, 'Books and Manuscripts,' in *Sir Hans Sloane: Collector, Scientist, Antiquary, Founding Father of the British Museum*, ed. by Arthur MacGregor (London: British Museum Press in Association with Alistair McAlpine for the Trustees of the British Museum, 1994), pp. 263–277 (p. 273); Julianne Simpson, 'From London to Toronto: A Case-Study of the Dispersal of Sloane's Library,' in *From Books to Bezoars: Sir Hans Sloane and His Collections*, ed. by Michael Hunter, Alison Walker and Arthur MacGregor (London: British Library, 2012), pp. 221–226. See also the essay by Alice Marples in this volume.

6 See, for some of these, Mark Purcell, *The Country House Library* (New Haven and London: Yale University Press for the National Trust, 2017). Books in the D'Israeli library are described in Marvin Spevack, 'The Library at Hughenden Manor,' *The Book Collector*, 59 (2010), 547–580 (at 560–572).

7 The remains of Isaac Williams's library, 215 volumes from the late eighteenth and early nineteenth centuries, are now at the University of Wales, Trinity St David (St David's College Lampeter). Fox Talbot's library is a working one, held at Lacock Abbey in Wiltshire (mentioned in one sentence in Mark Purcell, 'Libraries at Lacock Abbey,' *National Trust Historic Houses and Collections Annual* (2012), 36–43 (at 42)). Shaw's, which contains many presentation copies and multiple editions of Shaw's own work among its 2,800 or so titles, is at his home in Ayot St Lawrence.

8 See Karen Attar, 'More than a Mythologist: Jacob Bryant as Book Collector,' *The Library*, 3 (2002), 351–366 (at 355–356); E. Davis Coakley, 'Edward Worth and His Library,' in *The Alchemy of Medicine and Print: The Edward Worth Library, Dublin*, ed. by Danielle Westerhof (Dublin: Four Courts Press, 2010), pp. 36–47 (at p. 47).

9 See Karen Attar, *Directory*, pp. 21, 281, 356, 382 and 459. The Edinburgh material is discussed briefly in S. M. Simpson, 'The History of the Library 1837–1939,' in *Edinburgh University Library 1580–1980: A Collection of Historical Essays*, ed. by Jean R. Guild and Alexander Law (Edinburgh: Edinburgh University Library, 1982), pp. 94–114 (at pp. 101–102) and M. C. T. Simpson, 'The Special Collections,' in *Edinburgh University Library 1580–1980: A Collection of Historical Essays*, ed. by Jean R. Guild and Alexander Law (Edinburgh: Edinburgh University Library, 1982), pp. 140–162 (at p. 155). The Brighton and Hove material comprises about 1,000 volumes of Shakespeareana, from the late sixteenth to the late nineteenth century; the material at Chetham's Library, 3,500 single-sheet publications, mainly from the seventeenth and eighteenth centuries.

10 For the Spanish books, see P. E. Noble, 'Edward Phelips and the Eliot-Phelips Collection,' in *Grandeurs of Spain: The Eliot-Phelips Collection in the University of London Library, Journal of the Institute of Romance Studies* (2001), 13–20. For the erotica, see Paul J. Cross, 'The Private Case: A History,' in *The Library of the British Museum: Retrospective Essays on the Department of Printed Books*, ed. by P. R. Harris (London: British Library, 1991), pp. 201–240 (at p. 213).

11 For the books and the sale, see Mary Hobbs, 'The Cathedral Library,' in *Chichester Cathedral: An Historical Survey*, ed. by Mary Hobbs (Chichester: Phillimore, 1994), pp. 171–188 (at pp. 174–177 and 183–187) and, for the sale, Mary Hobbs, 'Books in Crisis,' *The Book Collector*, 44 (1995), 37–50. A few of King's books are among the Chichester Collection of books purchased from the sale at Senate House Library, University of London. Others, not so grouped, are at the University of Bristol Library.

12 See K. E. Attar, 'George Thackeray of King's College, Cambridge,' *The Book Collector*, 54 (2005), 389–407 (especially pp. 404 and 406). It remains common practice for libraries to cherry-pick donations to avoid duplication with existing holdings, or to refuse donations which donors wish to be kept intact and which have a high level of duplication with existing holdings.

13 Dibdin in 1809 listed large paper copies (equated with limited editions), illustrated (i.e. extra-illustrated) copies, unique copies, copies printed upon vellum, first editions (and specifically Shakespeare's First Folio and Greek and Latin classics), true editions (i.e. editions with variants), unopened copies and to an extent black letter, and further noted books printed by Caxton and Wynkyn de Worde and Aldines (Thomas Frognall Dibdin, *The Bibliomania or Book Madness, Containing Some Account of the History, Symptoms and Cure of this Fatal Disease*, ed. by Peter Danckwerts (Richmond: Tiger of the Stripe, 2007), pp. 56–74). See also John Carter, *Taste & Technique in Book Collecting*, 3rd ed. (London: Private Libraries Association, 1970), p. 21.

14 Alfred W. Pollard, 'Book-Collecting,' in *Encyclopaedia Britannica*, 11th ed., 29 vols. (Cambridge: Cambridge University Press, 1910–11), IV (1910), pp. 221–225 (at p. 224). John Carter wrote more bluntly: 'The variety of book-collecting, indeed, is almost infinite,' John Carter, *Books and Book-Collectors* (London: R. Hart-Davis, 1956), p. 11. Carter elsewhere lists popular collecting subjects at various times: see Carter, *Taste & Technique*, pp. 21–27.

15 Artillery and fortification constitute the subject of a special collection of over 500 early books, handbooks and drill manuals at the Royal Armouries Museum in Fareham; bagpipe and fiddle music mainly of the eighteenth and nineteenth centuries that of a bequest by Scottish teacher and composer John Murdoch Henderson (1902–1972) to the National Library of Scotland; there is a Miss Great Britain collection of over 1,000 images and pieces of ephemera from the competitions held between approximately 1950 and 1980 at Morecambe Library; and a special collection on the Titanic is held within the Maritime Collection at Southampton Central Library.

16 The most significant of these consists of some 4,000 plays printed between 1700 and 1900 collected by the French collector, actor and playwright Amédée Marandet, held at the University of Warwick (see School of Modern Languages and Cultures, University of Warwick, 'The Marandet Collection of French Plays,' www2.warwick.ac.uk/fac/arts/modernlanguages/marandet/ (accessed 12 October 2017); Jean Emelina and Peter Larkin, *Guide to the Marandet Collection of French Plays Held in the University of Warwick Library* (Coventry: University of Warwick Library, 1979)), followed by John Geoffrey Aspin's collection of about 1,400 seventeenth- and early eighteenth-century titles at Trinity College Dublin.

17 All three appear in the list of collecting topics of W. Carew Hazlitt, *The Book Collector: A General Survey of the Pursuit and of Those Who Have Engaged in It at Home and Abroad from the Earliest Period to the Present Time*

(London: J. Grant, 1904), p. 60; reproduced in Carter, *Taste & Technique*, p. 27. Carrying the interest forward, the Bible merits a chapter in Grant Uden, *Understanding Book-Collecting* (Woodbridge: Antique Collectors Club, 1982).

18 An ongoing 'Coronation collection' at Westminster Abbey of three hundred volumes from the seventeenth century onwards of primary printed sources and secondary material relating to the history, organization and significance of the English coronation ceremony is clearly part of its printed archive of business activity.

19 Percy H. Muir, 'The Nature and Scope of Book-Collecting,' in P. H. Muir et al., *Talks on Book Collecting*, ed. by P. H. Muir (London: Cassell, 1952), pp. 1–23 (at p. 7).

20 The Yule Collection is described in: J. C. T. Oates, 'The G. U. Yule Collection of the *Imitatio Christi* in the Library of St John's College,' *Transactions of the Cambridge Bibliographical Society*, 1 (1949), 88–90. Storr's concordance is: R. Storr, *Concordance to the Latin Original of the Four Books Known as De Imitatione Christi Given to the World A.D. 1441 by Thomas à Kempis* (Oxford: H. Frowde, Oxford University Press, 1910).

21 The exception is of 58 editions amassed by historian John Williams Williams, presented to St Andrews University. The Madan collections are at Cambridge University Library (65 volumes), Windsor Castle (about 70 volumes) and the British Library (133 volumes). For the British Library collection, see 'Notable Acquisitions,' *British Museum Quarterly*, 26 (1962), 57–58 and 64.

22 Non-literary authors to constitute the subject of collections include Charles Darwin (collections of between 485 and 600 volumes collected by the evolutionary embryologist Sir Gavin Rylands de Beer (King's College London), Zoology lecturer Sydney Smith (St Catharine's College, Cambridge) and Jack Johns (University of Kent), the Swiss theologian Karl Barth (Aberdeen University), the philosopher Emanuel Swedenborg (the Swedenborg Society Library; Chetham's Library, Manchester; and the Mitchell Library, Glasgow) and Isaac Newton (Royal Society Library). Analogous with single-author collections are the less common collections around a single musical composer (Beethoven; Mozart).

23 *A Directory of Rare Book and Special Collections in the United Kingdom and Republic of Ireland*, 2nd ed., ed. by B. C. Bloomfield with the assistance of Karen Potts (London: Library Association Publishing, 1997).

24 For the Cambridge collection, see 'The Phyllis T. M. Davies Collection of Walter de la Mare,' Cambridge University Library, *Newsletter*, 12 (1999), www.lib.cam.ac.uk/Newsletters/nl12/#de_la_mare (accessed 18 October 2017). The de la Mare working library is described and listed in: Giles de la Mare, 'The Walter de la Mare Library,' *Walter de la Mare Society Magazine*, 11 (2008), 3–47 and 'The Walter de la Mare Working Library: 2011 Addendum,' *Walter de la Mare Society Magazine*, 15 (2013), 38–43. There is some information about the editions of de la Mare's works at Senate House Library in K. E. Attar, 'Modern Special Collections Cataloguing: A University of London Case Study,' *Journal of Librarianship and Information Science*, 45 (2013), 168–176.

25 John L. Thornton, *Selected Readings in the History of Librarianship*, 2nd ed. (London: Library Association, 1966), p. 180.

26 Examples of local history collections made by individuals include the two local history collections on Yorkshire at Bradford Local Studies Library, made by the local historian James Norton Dickons and by local language teacher and antiquary Charles A. Federer (1837–1908), and collections made by the medical

practitioner Joseph Hambly Rowe (augmented by Edmund Hambly), mining historian Kenneth Hamilton Jenkin and local historian Ashley Rowe, at the Cornish Studies Library in Redruth. For examples of such collections beyond the public library sphere, see a diverse range of material on Norfolk history amassed by Norfolk scholar Robert W. Ketton-Cremer and bequeathed to the University of East Anglia (approximately one thousand volumes); a Yorkshire collection of 1,600 books deposited by Raymond Burton at the University of York; and a Channel Islands Collection made by medieval historian John Le Patourel (1909–1981) to be found further away than the standard local history collection from the subject of the collection, at the University of Leeds.

27 The most important Yeats collection is his personal library at the National Library of Ireland (acquired in 2002). The other Yeats collections are the Eamonn Cantwell Collections at University College Cork (donated 2003) and the Michael C. Gilsenan Collection of W. B Yeats donated to the University of Limerick in 2014. Of six further collections that mention Yeats as a noteworthy element, three are Irish (the Joseph Harnett Collection at University College Dublin, the Cuala Press Collection at Trinity College Dublin and, in Northern Ireland, presentation copies at Mount Stewart, Newtownards). For MacDiarmid, see the Langholm Library in Dumfriesshire, in the University of the West of Scotland at Paisley, the books he owned at Edinburgh University Library, and editions of MacDiarmid's poetry annotated by W. R. Aitken at the National Library of Scotland.

28 See the Mitchell Library, Glasgow; Dunfermline Carnegie Library & Galleries; and the Robert Burns Birthplace Museum. The fourth collection is at the Linen Hall Library in Belfast. Collections on Robert Owen are at the Robert Owen Memorial Museum in Newtown and at the National Library of Wales.

29 For the Aberdeen collection, see Alison Lumsden, 'The Bernard C. Lloyd Walter Scott Collection,' in *The Library and Archive Collections of the University of Aberdeen: An Introduction and Description*, ed. by Iain Beavan, Peter Davidson and Jane Stevenson (Manchester: Manchester University Press with the University of Aberdeen, 2011), pp. 278–279. Smaller Scott collections are held in the Edinburgh & Scottish Collections at Edinburgh Central Library (1,500 volumes), the National Library of Scotland (115 volumes from the Abbotsford Collection; 82 titles in the Gilson Collection), and the University of Stirling (90 titles). Small Scott collections in England comprise a Scott collection of 287 volumes given by Sir Arthur (Salusbury) MacNalty (1880–1969) to University College London and some presentations from Scott at Barnard Castle in County Durham.

30 Carter, *Taste & Technique*, p. 27.

31 The major Bunyan collections, one of which contains approximately 2,500 volumes, are at the John Bunyan Museum and Library in Bedford (see Patricia Hurry and Alan F. Cirket, *Bunyan Meeting Museum Library Catalogue* (Bedford: Bunyan Meeting Free Church, 1995)), with a further collection of 700 items at Bedford Central Library (see Richard Offor, 'The Offor Bunyan Books at Elstow,' *Library Association Record*, 62.4 (April 1960), 117–125; H. G. Tibbutt, 'Bunyan Libraries,' *Bedfordshire Magazine*, 15 (1975), 55–57). The third, markedly smaller, collection is Sir (Robert) Leicester Harmsworth's collection (239 volumes) at the British Library; see H. M. Nixon, 'Bunyan Editions from the Library of Sir Leicester Harmsworth,' *British Museum Quarterly*, 15 (1941–50), 17–18. Bunyan forms a component of broader Puritan collections at the Evangelical Library (London); Regent's Park College, Oxford; and Caleb

Robjohns's collection at the University of Leicester. Canterbury Christ Church University purchased a fourth, smaller collection (about 120 volumes). Whilst Elizabeth Gaskell is prominent within broader special collections at the Universities of Leeds and St Andrews, the main collection devoted solely to her is held at Manchester Central Library (approximately 950 items: for the post-1945 acquisitions within it, see Christine Lingard, 'The Gaskell Collection in Manchester Central Library,' *Gaskell Society Journal*, 2 (1989), 59–75), with smaller Gaskell collections at the John Rylands Library in Manchester (approximately 250 volumes, including editions from the library of Gaskell scholar John Geoffrey Sharps (1936–2006)) and Knutsford Library (approximately 200 volumes collected by Archie Stanton Whitfield, author of *Mrs Gaskell: Her Life and Work*). Canterbury Christ Church University purchased a collection of approximately 120 volumes between about 1995 and 2015. The major Bewick collections are at Bewick's childhood home of Cherrybrook, Mickley (c. 450 items) and Newcastle City Library (over 600 volumes given by a local Victorian businessman, John William Pease), with a smaller collection at Newcastle University and an unspecified quantity of items within the Natural History Society of Northumbria Library.

32 The Bolton physician John Johnston (d. 1918) collected Whitman as the basis of a 2,000-item strong Walt Whitman collection at Bolton Library and Museum Services, with a smaller collection assembled by Charles Frederick Sixsmith (1871–1953) of Lancashire and Charles E. Feinberg of Detroit at the John Rylands Library, Manchester. Both collections include American input. The Cardiff lecturer Benjamin Joseph Morse (1878–1977) assembled a Rilke collection, which is at Cardiff University Library.

33 Arthurian material is also a strength within the Celtic Studies collection at Cardiff University Library.

34 Glasgow Life, 'Hillhouse Collection,' www.glasgowlife.org.uk/libraries/the-mitchell-library/special-collections/hillhouse/pages/default.aspx (accessed 9 October 2017); David Parlett, *The Oxford Dictionary of Board Games* (Oxford: Oxford University Press, 1999), p. 269.

35 John Ferriar, *The Bibliomania, an Epistle to Richard Heber* (London: T. Cadell and W. Davies, 1809), p. 4.

36 Andrew Lang, *Books and Bookmen* (London: Longmans, Green, 1886), pp. 103–104; Carter and Muir, looking back to the period, agree with him: see John Carter, *Books and Book Collectors*, p. 120; Muir, 'The Nature and Scope of Book Collecting,' p. 4.

37 Karen Attar, *Directory*, pp. 328–329 (Paget Toynbee) and 299 (Fletcher); 'The presses of Aldus, Colinaeus, Stephanus, Turnebus and Elzevir are well represented by excellent copies of important works' (T. Percy C. Kirkpatrick, *The History of Doctor Steevens' Hospital, Dublin, 1720–1920* (Dublin: Dublin University Press, 1964), p. 64.

38 De Ricci, *English Collectors*, p. 159. De Ricci further notes the Aldines and Elzevirs in a collection formed by Haughton James in about 1790 (p. 99, n. 2).

39 In 1950 the Guildhall gave the collection to the University of London. See Jakob Harskamp, 'When Leiden Meets London: The Background of the ULL's Elzevier Collection,' *FULLview*, 21 (2002), 16–19; repr. as 'Elzevir in Central London,' www.senatehouselibrary.ac.uk/elzevir-central-london (accessed 9 October 2017).

40 Karen Attar, *Directory*, p. 17.

41 David McKitterick, 'Books and Other Collections,' in *The Making of the Wren Library, Trinity College, Cambridge*, ed. by David McKitterick (Cambridge: Cambridge University Press, 1995), pp. 50–109 (at p. 92).
42 The Bodleian Library regarded Tauchnitz books as noteworthy enough to collocate its Tauchnitz books as a special collection from 1980 onwards, 'in order to facilitate its use, study and increase': see 'The Tauchnitz Edition,' *Bodleian Library Record*, 10 (1981), 210–211 (at 211).
43 Private presses from a collecting angle are the subject of a chapter of Uden, *Understanding Book Collecting*, pp. 84–97.
44 See Dorothy A. Harrop, *Catalogue of the William Ridler Collection of Fine Printing* (Birmingham: Birmingham City Council, Public Libraries Department, 1989).
45 See G. Breeze, 'The Emery Walker Library,' *Printing Historical Society Bulletin*, 31 (1991), 3–5.
46 See Mark Purcell, William Hale and David Pearson, *Treasures from Lord Fairhaven's Library at Anglesey Abbey* (London: Scala, 2013); Frank Stubbings, *The Graham Watson Collection of Colour Plate Books at Emmanuel College, Cambridge* (Cambridge: Emmanuel College, 1993).
47 Arnold's collection is now at the British Library and Radford's at the Bodleian Library. See Edward Arnold, *A Catalogue of the Library Formed by Edward Arnold* (Dorking: Privately Printed, 1921); Clive Hurst, 'Collection of Miniature Books,' *Bodleian Library Record*, 23 (2010), 249.
48 See especially Mirjam M. Foot, *The Henry Davis Gift: A Collection of Bookbindings*, 3 vols. (London: British Library, 1978–2010). A smaller bequest from Henry Davis at the University of Ulster, Coleraine, is of early printed books rather than bindings: see Benedikt S. Benedikz, *The Ulster Gift: Books Presented to the University of Ulster* (Coleraine: University of Ulster, 1990); H. A. Feisenberger, 'The Henry Davis Collection II: The Ulster Gift,' *The Book Collector*, 21 (1972), 339–355.
49 Tim Gulliford, 'Bound by Alvah Cook, Bath's Mysterious Binder,' *The Bookbinder*, 19 (2005), 43–46.
50 See also 1,100 volumes of regency bindings from the Royal Pavilion in Brighton, now at Brighton & Hove City Libraries. These should be seen as books bound in the fashionable style of the time rather than a collection of bindings as such.
51 Karen Attar, *Directory*, p. 37. Hugh Frederick Hornby bequeathed to what is now Liverpool Central Library some 8,000 rare volumes, focusing on deluxe and limited editions, usually illustrated and finely bound, with many large paper copies. See Henry E. Curran and Charles Robertson, *Ex Bibliotheca Hugh Frederick Hornby: Catalogue of the Art Library Bequeathed by Hugh Frederick Hornby Esq. to the Free Public Library of the City of Liverpool* (Liverpool: Library, Museum and Arts Committee, 1906).
52 'Now history' collections of the Civil War are present at Lincoln Cathedral (3,000 pamphlets from the collection of Michael Honywood (1597–1681), Dean of Lincoln from 1660, among the 5,000 books he gave the cathedral); the Bodleian Library (from the bequest of Thomas Barlow [1607–1691], Bishop of Lincoln); and Worcester College, Oxford (the library of Sir William Clarke (1623/4–1666). See also the collections of John Robartes, 1st Earl of Radnor, at Lanhydrock (Purcell, *The Country House Library*, p. 95). Contemporaneous collections pertaining to the First World War include the

theologian William Sanday's (1843–1920) bequest to the Queen's College, Oxford (approximately 700 pamphlets) and the 1914–1918 War Collection at University College London (over 1,800 items) bequeathed by the writer, translator and textual scholar Leonard Arthur Magnus (1879–1924), and most spectacularly that made by University Librarian Francis Jenkinson for Cambridge University Library (about 10,000 items; see Hugh Fraser Stewart, *Francis Jenkinson, Fellow of Trinity College Cambridge and University Librarian: A Memoir* [Cambridge: Cambridge University Press, 1926], pp. 140–142). Contemporaneous collecting of printed material pertaining to the Second World War among the various special collections devoted to the Second World War is harder to distinguish, beyond acquisitions of Nazi books made shortly after the War (e.g., the Nazi Collection at Manchester Central Library and, comprising or including National Socialist books for children, the SHAEF Collection at the British Library; the EPCOM Collection at Senate House Library, University of London; and the National Socialist Collection acquired through HMSO at Cambridge University Library). It may also be assumed for collections at the Wiener Library (see Ben Barkow, *Alfred Wiener and the Making of the Holocaust Library* (London: V. Mitchell, 1997). Collecting on the World Wars may be less well documented in special collections than it is in fact, because such books, unlike seventeenth-century pamphlets, are likely to be part of general collections.

53 See James Hinton, *The Mass Observers: A History* (Oxford: Oxford University Press, 2013), p. 140.

54 Among collections devoted to or including the Great Exhibition, collections were made contemporaneously by the Exhibition's commissioner, John Scott Russell (Royal Society of Arts) and by the art patron and Exhibition co-organizer Sir Charles Wentworth Dilke (1810–1869) at the National Art Library.

55 See Michael Mendle, 'George Thomason's Intentions,' in Mandelbrote and Taylor, *Libraries within the Library*, pp. 171–186; *Catalogue of the Pepys Library at Magdalene College, Cambridge, vol. 2: Ballads*, compiled by Helen Weinstein, 2 vols. (Cambridge: Brewer, 1992–1994).

56 Geoffrey Keynes, *A Bibliography of Dr. John Donne, Dean of Saint Paul's* (Cambridge: Baskerville Club, 1914); *A Bibliography of Dr. Robert Hooke* (Oxford: Clarendon Press, 1960); *A Bibliography of George Berkeley, Bishop of Cloyne: His Works and His Critics in the Eighteenth Century* (Oxford: Clarendon Press, 1976); *A Bibliography of Henry King* (London: D. Cleverdon, 1977); *A Bibliography of Rupert Brooke* (London: R. Hart-Davis, 1954); *A Bibliography of Siegfried Sassoon* (London: R. Hart-Davis, 1962); *A Bibliography of Sir Thomas Browne, Kt, M. D.* (Cambridge: Cambridge University Press, 1924); *A Bibliography of Sir William Petty, F. R. S., and Observations on the Bills of Mortality by John Graunt, F. R. S.* (Oxford: Clarendon Press, 1971); *A Bibliography of the Writings of William Harvey, M. D., Discoverer of the Circulation of the Blood* (Cambridge: Cambridge University Press, 1928); *A Bibliography of William Blake* (New York: Grolier Club, 1921); *Bibliography of William Hazlitt* (London: Nonesuch Press, 1931); *Dr. Martin Lister: A Bibliography* (Godalming: St Pauls Bibliographies, 1981); *Dr. Timothie Bright, 1550–1615: A Survey of His Life with a Bibliography of His Writings* (London: Wellcome Historical Medical Library, 1962); *Jane Austen: A Bibliography* (London: Nonesuch Press, 1929); *John Evelyn: A Study in Bibliophily & a Bibliography of His Writings* (Cambridge: Cambridge University Press, 1937); *John Ray: A*

Bibliography (London: Faber & Faber, 1951). Keynes also edited works by and about John Donne, Rupert Brooke, Thomas Browne, Samuel Butler, William Hazlitt, and especially William Blake, and wrote about William Harvey. For Keynes's own library, see Geoffrey Keynes, *Bibliotheca Bibliographici: A Catalogue of the Library Formed by Geoffrey Keynes* (London: Trianon Press, 1964; lists about half the items in the library). A brief overview of the collections is available at: www.lib.cam.ac.uk/collections/special-collections/collections/collection-name/keynes

57 J. H. P. Pafford, 'Historical Introduction,' in *University of London Library, Catalogue of the Goldsmiths' Library of Economic Literature, vol. 1: Printed Books to 1800*, ed. by Margaret Canney and David Knott (London: Cambridge University Press, 1970; repr. London: Athlone Press, 1982), pp. ix–xviii (at p. ix).

58 Alexander Gordon, *Family History of the Lawrences of Cornwall* (West Norwood: Privately Printed, 1915), p. 2 of pref. (unpaginated).

59 *Early English Books Online* was launched only in 1998, *Eighteenth-Century Collections Online* in 2003, and Google Books in 2011, with new digitization projects, such as *Early European Books*, constantly underway. For an overview of some of the smaller digitization projects of rare materials, see K. E. Attar, 'Rare Book Librarianship and Historical Bibliography,' in *British Librarianship and Information Work 2006–2010*, ed. by J. H. Bowman (London: J. H. Bowman, 2012), pp. 184–206 (at pp. 190–192) and in *British Librarianship and Information Work 2011–2015*, ed. by J. H. Bowman (London: J. H. Bowman, 2017), pp. 216–238 (at pp. 218–220).

60 See David Pearson, *Books as History* (London: British Library, 2008), ch. 6, 'The Collective Value of Libraries' (pp. 163–173). Pearson discusses annotation more at the level of famous people annotating specific books (pp. 93–139).

61 Betjeman's library comprises over 4,000 books and pamphlets, many annotated by Betjeman, from the eighteenth to the twentieth centuries; von Hügel's some 3,600 works on philosophy, religion and history, mainly of the nineteenth and twentieth centuries; and Bell's about 1,500 items of papyrological texts and studies and background material on the history and literature of the ancient world. See Karen Attar, *Directory*, pp. 71, 500, and 507 respectively.

62 See Karen Attar, *Directory*, pp. 22, 282, 498, 469.

63 See Karen Attar, *Directory*, p. 483. This collection currently comprises approximately 200 volumes. The National Library of Scotland similarly collects miniature books with a Scottish connection: see National Library of Scotland, 'Miniature Books,' www.nls.uk/collections/rare-books/collections/miniature-books (accessed 7 November 2017). Note also a collection of small books in various languages and on various subjects, printed between the sixteenth and the twentieth centuries, assembled by the London Library (Karen Attar, *Directory*, p. 199).

64 Particularly good examples are at Manchester Metropolitan University and Chelsea College of Arts at the University of the Arts, with smaller collections at Goldsmiths, University of London; Oxford Brookes University; the Scottish National Galleries; Cardiff Metropolitan University; and Leeds College of Art.

65 See Karen Attar, *Directory*, pp. 19–21 (quotation on p. 19). Alison Cullingford expands upon the Bradford policy in Alison Cullingford, *The Special Collections Handbook*, 2nd ed. (London: Facet Publishing, 2016), p. 84.

66 The Eleanor Farjeon Collection is now in Camden Local Studies and Archives Centre.

67 The 'unique and distinctive' agenda was highlighted in a strategic strand of RLUK activity 2011–2014: see RLUK (Research Libraries UK), 'Promoting Unique and Distinctive Collections,' www.rluk.ac.uk/strategicactivity/strategic-strands/udc/ and Alison Cullingford, 'Unique and Distinctive Collections: Opportunities for Research Libraries,' ed. by Caroline Peach and Mike Mertens (Research Libraries UK, 2014), www.rluk.ac.uk/wp-content/uploads/2014/12/RLUK-UDC-Report.pdf (both accessed 3 September 2016). For a summary from an American perspective of special collections making libraries distinctive, see Donald J. Waters, 'The Changing Role of Special Collections in Scholarly Communications.' Presented at Fall Forum hosted by the Association of Research Libraries and the Coalition for Networked Information on *An Age of Discovery: Distinctive Collections in the Digital Age*. Washington, DC, October 14, 2009, p. 3, http://msc.mellon.org/staff-papers/specialcollectionsvalue.pdf (accessed 14 November 2017).

68 A. N. L. Munby, 'Floreat Bibliomania,' in *Essays and Papers*, p. 39.

69 See 'Notable Accessions,' *Bodleian Library Record*, 12 (1986), 142–150 (at 145–147); D. I. Masson, *Catalogue of the Romany Collection Formed by D.U. McGregor Phillipps* … (Edinburgh: T. Nelson for the Brotherton Collection, 1962).

70 Karen Attar, *Directory*, pp. 551–571 (index of collectors).

71 For collections given by academic women to their own institutions, see especially the Christina Roaf Collection of Italian books at Somerville College Oxford; Marjorie Reeve's collection on Abbot Joachim of Fiore and on prophecy and millenarianism at St Anne's College, Oxford; and Catherine Cooke's collection of items on Russian and Soviet architecture and design (c. 1,300 items) at Cambridge University Library. For a large collection given outside academia, see Marie Stopes's collection of over 3,000 items, chiefly pamphlets and ephemera pertaining to birth control, medical and social subjects (1861–1958), at the British Library. The largest twenty-first-century example of a more diversely employed female academic's collections is that of some 2,000 twentieth-century books and pamphlets on the history of labour and working life in the Caribbean and Central America, collected by Mary Turner (1931–2013), an Englishwoman who became Professor of History at Dalhousie University, Canada, which are now in the Bishopsgate Institute, London.

72 About 30 linear metres and 5,000 volumes respectively. Smaller collections of female food writers are those of Elizabeth David (approximately 750 books from the nineteenth and twentieth centuries) and Mary Wondrausch (about 150 books from the same period), both at the Guildhall Library, London.

73 Note also Ann Hutchinson Guest's 2,000 books from the nineteenth and twentieth centuries on labonotation at the University of Roehampton, Mary Anne Chapman's collection of about 1,400 nineteenth-century plays given to the Guildhall in 1895, and over 1,500 items on Oscar Wilde and his associates collected by Mary, Viscountess Eccles, and bequeathed to the British Library in 2003 (see Andrea Lloyd, 'The Lady Eccles Oscar Wilde Collection,' *Electronic British Library Journal* (2010), art. 3, 1–13, www.bl.uk/eblj/2010articles/pdf/ebljarticle32010.pdf (accessed 11 November 2017)). A large library (in terms of female ownership) of miscellaneous books which was institutionalized as a collection is that of the author and Egyptologist Amelia B. Edwards (1831–1892) of some 5,000 books at Somerville College, Oxford.

74 Anne Renier, 'The Renier Collection of Children's Books,' *The Book Collector*, 23 (1974), 40–52. Smaller collections of children's books given by a husband and wife are the Parker Collection of Early Children's Books at the Library of Birmingham, over 4,600 volumes given by Mr and Mrs J. F. Parker, and about 300 early nineteenth-century children's books given to the University of Reading in the 1950s by Sir Frank and Lady Stenton; whether Mrs Parker and Lady Stenton were active collectors is less clear.

75 David Barrett, *Catalogue of the Wardrop Collection and of Other Georgian Books and Manuscripts in the Bodleian Library* (Oxford: Oxford University Press for the Marjory Wardrop Fund, 1973).

76 Collections on Dada and Dundee are among the larger ones: the art collector Gabrielle Keiller's collection of 1,050 books and periodicals, mainly rare or limited editions, on Dada and surrealism is at the Scottish National Gallery of Modern Art, and Catherine M. Kinnear donated most of the 4,600 items in the Kinnear Local Collection at Dundee University Library. Lucy Ethel Willcock bequeathed early editions of Dante, a long-standing collecting subject, to Lady Margaret Hall, Oxford, in 1919.

77 The needlework collection comprises some 300 nineteenth- and twentieth-century books, pamphlets and journals on embroidery, needlework, lace-making and related crafts, collected by Valda Cowie, at the University of Reading. But note that the only collection devoted to baking and confectionary (2,837 items) is from a man, Joseph Hancock Macadam, President of the Scottish Association of Master Bakers, who bequeathed it to the National Library of Scotland.

78 Other female collectors of music with items in special collections include Lydia Acland (1786–1856), whose music is at Killerton House, a National Trust property in Exeter; Patricia Gilbert, who collected 280 pieces of sheet music from the nineteenth and twentieth centuries now at the University of Bristol; the music teacher Sophie Weisse, whose 600 or so books and scores relating to Beethoven are at Edinburgh University Library and Peggy Seeger, whose books and scores are merged with those of her husband, Ewan MacColl, at Goldsmiths', University of London.

79 For a description of Pollard's collection, see Lydia Ferguson, 'Cultivating Childhood: The Pollard Collection of Children's Books,' in *The Old Library, Trinity College Dublin, 1712–2012*, ed. by W. E. Vaughan (Dublin: Four Courts Press, 2012), pp. 190–209.

80 Other collections include 230 children's books collected by Sarah Chorley, at Newcastle University; 200 titles c. 1784–1865 collected by Mabel Irene Martin (d. 1982) at Senate House Library, University of London; a collection made by Marianne Hugon (1881–1952) now at St Anne's College, Oxford; and 91 books from Miss G. E. Brereton and Mrs G. M. Mayne at St Hilda's College, Oxford.

81 *A Chaplet for Charlotte Yonge*, ed. by Georgina Battiscombe and Marghanita Laski (London: Cresset, 1965). Laski's collection is at her alma mater, Somerville College Oxford. The other Yonge collections are at Lady Margaret Hall, Oxford (formed by Mrs C. S. Unwin and Mrs M. Dunlop) and at Girton College, Cambridge (donor not stated).

82 Collections of ephemera are most pronounced at the British Library, because the British Library has taken particular care to record them (see Karen Attar, *Directory*, pp. 140–147). The British Library is the home of Olga Hirsch's collection of over 3,500 sheets of decorated paper: see Mirjam M. Foot, 'The Olga

Hirsch Collection of Decorated Papers,' *Electronic British Library Journal* (1981), art. 2, 12–38, www.bl.uk/eblj/1981articles/pdf/article2.pdf (acccessed 11 November 2017). It also houses general ephemera collated by Sarah Sophia Banks (1744–1818), pertaining mainly to her times (see also the chapter by Arlene Leis in this volume), as well as London and continental theatre programmes, 1932–1974, assembled by Diana Gordon (the London ones are described in the online database 'Concert Programmes,' www.concertprogrammes.org.uk (accessed 13 November 2017)) and ephemera relating to the women's suffrage movement in England accumulated by the activist Maud Arncliffe Sennett (1862–1936). A collection of ephemera formed by a woman and held elsewhere is Elspeth Evans's collections of advertisements pertaining to the arts in London from the 1960s to the 1990s (approximately 100 boxes at the University of Reading). For the John Johnson collection, see Bodleian Libraries, University of Oxford, 'John Johnson Collection of Printed Ephemera,' www.bodleian.ox.ac.uk/johnson (accessed 15 November 2017).

83 See Henry Guppy, *The John Rylands Library, Manchester, 1899–1935: A Brief Record of Its History with Descriptions of the Building and its Contents* (Manchester: Manchester University Press, 1935), pp. 6–16; John R. Hodgson, *A Guide to the Special Collections of the John Rylands University Library of Manchester* (Manchester: John Rylands University Library, 1999); *Riches of the Rylands: The Special Collections of the University of Manchester Library* (Manchester: Manchester University Press, 2015), pp. 1–6.

84 See 'Law Society Defies Scholars with Mendham Collection Auction,' *The Guardian* (3 June 2013), www.theguardian.com/books/2013/jun/03/law-society-mendham-collection-auction (accessed 22 September 2016). Shorter accounts are available in *The Book Collector*, 61 (2012), 523–524 and 62 (2013), 397.

85 The Brenchley T. S. Eliot Collection (approximately 530 titles, bequeathed in 2011) and the Neil Ritchie Sitwell Collection (approximately 1,908 titles, bequeathed in 2012) are both at Merton College, Oxford. The M. S. Anderson Collection of Writings on Russia Printed Between 1525 and 1917, comprising some 1,850 titles, was given to Senate House Library, University of London, in 2008; see Karen Attar, 'The M. S. Anderson Collection of Writings on Russia Printed Between 1525 and 1917: An Introduction,' *Solanus*, 22 (2011), 63–78. Cambridge University acquired Gilbert de Botton's Montaigne collection in 2008: for a description and exhibition catalogue, see Philip Ford, *The Montaigne Library of Gilbert de Botton at Cambridge University Library* (Cambridge: Cambridge University Library, 2008).

Index

For Product Safety Concerns and Information please contact our EU
representative GPSR@taylorandfrancis.com
Taylor & Francis Verlag GmbH, Kaufingerstraße 24, 80331 München, Germany

www.ingramcontent.com/pod-product-compliance
Lightning Source LLC
LaVergne TN
LVHW020629100826
845148LV00012B/2103

* 9 7 8 0 3 6 7 6 0 6 8 0 0 *